The image shown on the cover was obtained using a Siemens Connectome 3T scanner based at the Massachusetts General Hospital (MGH) in Cambridge, MA as part of the MGH-USC Human Connectome Project (HCP). Using a method called diffusion imaging, it is possible to map the white matter fiber pathways that make up the neural connections between cortical areas of the brain. Here, the "white matter" fibers of the brain (with the occipital lobe on the left and the frontal lobe on the right) are color-coded to illustrate fiber directionality: green is oriented anterior-to-posterior in the brain; red fibers are oriented left-to-right; while, blue fibers are oriented inferior-to-superior. The image volume is "cut" sagittally through the right hemisphere in order to showcase the corpus callosum and the corona radiata. - Dr. John D. Van Horn

This is the SECOND EDITION of our book. Gaspard Mucundanyi, a doctoral research assistant and Karin Wiburg, distinguished professor in the College of Education, New Mexico State University, spent the summer of 2016 completing necessary edits that were not completed in the First Edition. We also made minor changes to ensure better formatting and correct references for all chapters. We also want to dedicate the second edition to J.T. Knight, one of the original editors, who sadly passed away soon after the EDLT 607 class ended and the first edition of the book was created.

We give Teachers the right to make free copies of any section of this book for their class members. This is a non-profit venture. Any monies received will be used for graduate student publications or travel.

ISBN# 9781537091808

i

Dedication

This second edition is dedicated to J.T. Knight, a graduate student and a lawyer, a great writer and colleague. At the time of his death he was working as a Technology Commercialization Associate for New Mexico State University's Arrowhead Center. He received his B.A. at Columbia University. He began his graduate studies at Pace University and earned a J.D. from the University of Wisconsin, Madison. His work on this book and his academic legacy has inspired us to write this second edition.

Table of Contents

Preface

This book is what happened when 10 doctoral students, their professor, and the professor's graduate assistant, in a class about learning, research and technology, began to discuss a meaningful project on learning theory that might be more useful than writing another paper for the teacher.

As the professor for the class I have the responsibility of ensuring that students meet the class learning goals resulting in each student's developing his or her own theoretical frameworks for learning and research. I also expected the students to integrate their theoretical frameworks with the affordance of technology to support learning. Since my own learning theory focuses on the benefits of engaged learning, the usefulness of problem-based projects for engaging learning, and the power of a social-constructivist learning environment, I had faith, after 40 years of teaching and research, that the students would learn best when provided opportunities to engage in personally and socially meaningful projects that involved sharing what they were learning.

So we discussed the problems we saw in current education, particularly an over-emphasis on testing. Many prevalent educational policies seemed to contradict what the students were learning about teaching for deep learning and having time for teachers to work together to study their teaching. We concluded that there was a great need for a simple, easy to read book, for both educators and the general public, that could inform people with well-documented writing on what learning theorists can teach us. Translated, of course, from educational jargon to well-defined English, and we wanted the book to be accessible to the public. Many of the students in my class also write and speak high-level Spanish so these writers might even translate this book into Spanish sometime for access in the border region. We began to talk about *the book* as a *Little Book of Learning Theories*. Students began the class by doing extensive research and reading of original learning pioneers from Montessori to Skinner to Vygotsky, worked in teams to group different learning theories into meaningful chunks, first for an academic paper and then to be translated into chapters in this little book.

The lead editor and professor for the class will follow this forward with the first chapter, a brief introduction of how learning theory has changed and evolved from the beginning of the 20th century to today. This will provide a framework to support the rest of the book. The professor will ensure that what is written for this book is grounded in research and understandable. The students have created narratives that are hopefully both informative and interesting. Happy reading!

We are currently creating a Second Edition of this book. In our haste to create this book the first time we found later some sections needed additional editing. We have worked to improve the format and to correct and complete references. I want to thank Gaspard Mucundanyi, a doctoral research assistant, a former assistant lecturer in Computer Science from Rwanda, Africa and currently a student of Curriculum & Instruction and Learning Design, for his additional work on this book.

Karin M. Wiburg, Ed.D. July 31, 2016

Chapter 1 - An Introduction to Learning Theory

Karin M. Wiburg

Our understanding of learning has evolved rapidly in the labs and symposiums of the learning theorists, or learning scientists, as they are now called but little of this knowledge has been communicated to the people who serve and are served by education. These people include the school administrator, the classroom teacher, the parent, the local politician, students and counselors and local citizens from all communities.

This chapter tells the story of how our perceptions of learning have changed over time in a way that will hopefully help the reader build a framework for learning and thinking about learning. This introduction begins with Skinner's radical reaction against the mystical and religious beliefs about learning and the nature of learners in the 19th century. People were classified as intelligent based on all kinds of beliefs from your religious and ethnic make-up to the shape of your head or the nature of your personality. The overview that I developed continues through the behaviorist period, into the cognitive revolution, and finally into a constructivist theory of knowledge creation. Somewhere during that journey, Robert Gagne came up with a theory of different types of learning and tied types of learning to different teaching strategies. A table summarizing Robert Gagne's theory of teaching for learning is included in this chapter. The chapter ends with an overview of the book and a brief summary of the contents of each chapter.

A psychological/biological perspective

In the late 19th century there was increased speculation about the causes of learning and theorists such as Sigmund Freud began to conceptualize different parts of the mind and their influences on behavior. This early learning theory around instincts, drives, and the workings of the subconscious mind is shown in the diagram below.

At the same time as the rise of psychology there was an equal growth in the belief that science can provide us with the way to learn and improve behavior and school success. In many ways the conflict between traditional positivistic *Science* (a belief in only the findings of realistic and controlled experiments) and *Philosophy* (an experienced teacher can tell you what her students know by interacting with and observing them) continues to this day. This conflict is seen in the tension between scientific testing of students on standardized tests and what students and teachers know that they know in real life. Over time educational policies have demonstrated swings between philosophical-epistemological beliefs, such as *whole language* and scientific beliefs, such as the use of *value-added scientific testing models* to evaluate students and teachers. It is possible to combine some of the strengths of both approaches by using qualitative and philosophical experiences and thoughts to begin to conceptualize model learning environments and to then to test approaches to learning by using more traditional quantitative research.

A psychological/biological perspective

A person learns because of innate drives, desires, and motivations that arise from biologically-based, psychological states. Unconscious thought may have more influence on behavior than conscious thought. Some theorists believe in genetic determinism.

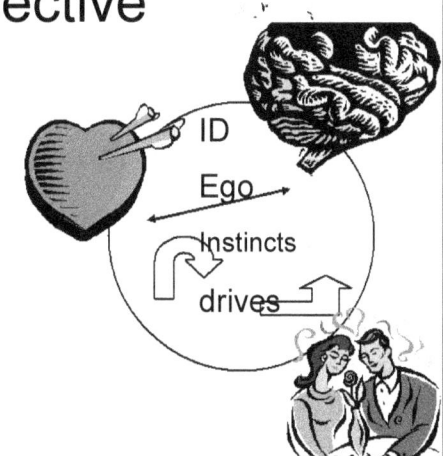

Selected theorists: Henri Rousseau, S. Freud, E. Erickson, Carl Jung, K. Horney, Carl Rogers, A. Maslow

In the 19th and early 20th century most of the theories of learning were based on either genetic determinism or philosophical beliefs about learning such as the influence of the personality or the mind. It was into this environment that Pavlov, Thorndike and others suggested the potential power of focusing on behavior itself rather than our philosophical beliefs about how people learn and how the mind works. While today there is much disdain for the old behavioral models, these ideas were innovative and break-through ideas in the early 20th century.

Behavioral Learning Theory

Behaviorist theory has had a long period of ascendance in psychology and education and is still used in learning designs, especially those involving students with special needs. The origin of behaviorism emerged in the labs of learning theorists such as John Watson, Ivan Pavlov, and Edward Thorndike, who were working on what has been called classical behaviorism. The most famous of these experiments was Pavlov's noticing that the ringing of a bell seemed to stir up hunger in dogs after the ringing was paired with feeding. We are not immune to classical conditioning especially when passing an ice cream or chocolate store on a walk. Suddenly the saliva and the hunger pains can be felt by many people.

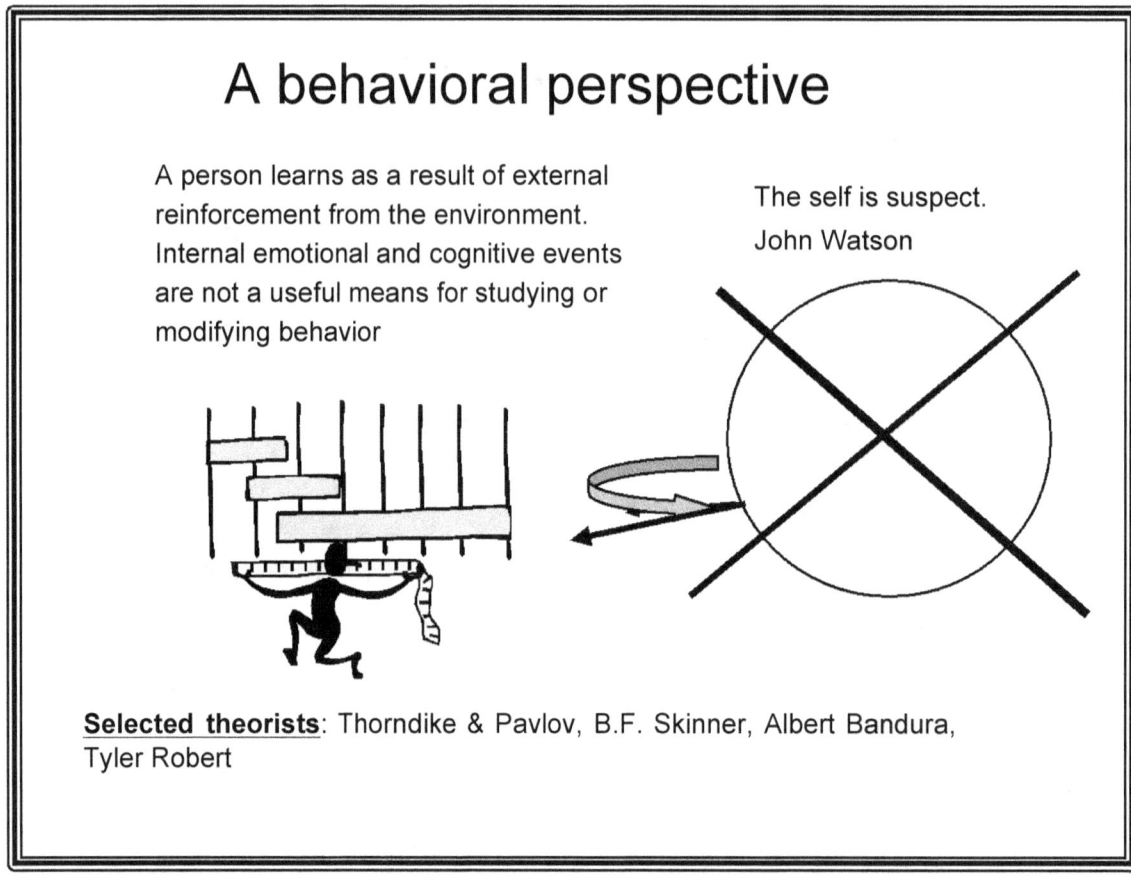

A behavioral perspective

A person learns as a result of external reinforcement from the environment. Internal emotional and cognitive events are not a useful means for studying or modifying behavior

The self is suspect.
John Watson

Selected theorists: Thorndike & Pavlov, B.F. Skinner, Albert Bandura, Tyler Robert

However, the real power of behavioral theory for controlling learning and actions began when Skinner proposed allowing random behavior to occur until the teacher or psychologist saw a behavior they liked and started to reward the behavior they wanted. This was called operant conditioning and involved positive reinforcement. If a reward was removed from an unwanted behavior this was called negative reinforcement.

Using behaviorism to control behavior is usually quite effective. The fact that it works can also be a problem for teachers. During the heaviest use of behaviorist theory in schools, teachers began to believe they, and not the student, were responsible for how well the student performed. This resulted in some teachers feeling guilty when students had trouble learning, and some students and parents blaming ONLY the teacher for their child's lack of learning, and a lack of responsibility by the learner for her/his own learning.

We now know from cognitive learning theory that the more effort the learner puts into the task of learning, especially deeper learning like problem-solving, the more the learning lasts and is later retrievable from long-term memory and useful in further learning. Rewards will always have a place in learning, but the use of a more cognitive approach might help students feel more internal satisfaction when solving a problem or putting ideas together. This leads to a more internal locus of control on the part of the student who may need less external controls (at least in theory).

Cognitive Learning Theory

In the 1960s and 70s people began to wonder why so many different kinds of behavior could not be explained by a simple behavior-reinforcement theory. Noam Chomsky introduced the notion of a language acquisition device that we all seem to be born with, something inherent to the brain. Other psychologists questioned whether simple reinforcement could support highly complex human thinking and problem-solving. Experiments, such as the famous marshmallow experiments at Stanford, showed that what people individually believe influences their behavior as much or more than what the environment is reinforcing.

The outcomes of reinforcements in complex settings differed depending on the individual or group. Something happened between the behavior, the reinforcement, and the next behavior, something that might have to do with the processing in the mind.

A cognitive perspective

A person learns as a result of <u>her/his perceptions and understanding</u> of the environment. It is most useful to focus on the internal cognitive and affective processes in the person in response to environmental interactions

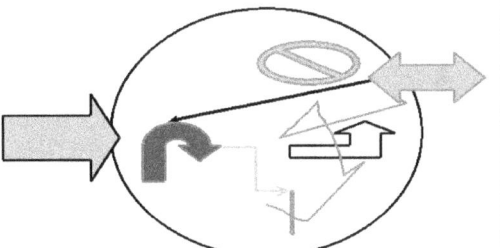

<u>Selected theorists</u>: Jean Piaget , Laurence Kohlberg , Merlin C. Wittrock, Karl H. Pribram , J. P. Guilford; Robert J Sternberg, Howard Gardner, Robert Gagne, Noam Chomsky

Constructivist Learning Theory

It may have been partially the growth in technology and the potential of the computer that supported a move toward understanding the setting in which cognition occurred. It seemed that elements of the environment were influencing learning as much as individual cognitive processing. It was at this time that ideas related to situated cognition and contextual and social learning theories emerged. The constructivist notion is that the learner creates knowledge as he or she makes meaning of the learning opportunities presented to them.

A constructivist perspective

A person learns as a result of how he/she cognitively constructs interactions with people, tools, and culture. Important mediating factors are the socio-cultural environment and the affordance of the tools and learning environment. <u>Constructivism</u> is a theory of how knowledge is constructed. <u>Constructionism</u> requires artifacts to assist learning (Papert, and the MIT research group)

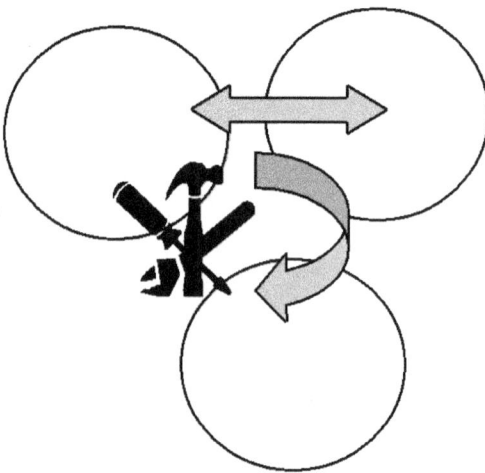

<u>Selected theorists</u>:Lev Vygotsky, Seymour Papert, Cathrine Fosnot, Michael Cole, Peg Griffin, Jim Wertsch, Ann Brown, Luis Moll, Karin Wiburg, James Gee

Critical Pedagogy

There is a lot of talk about the need for critical pedagogy in current calls for educational reform. Critical pedagogy is a philosophy of teaching, which is based on understanding the positions of power in society that influence educational thought and practice. This approach, which is not really a learning theory, asks learners to reflect critically on education and think about who is privileged in the current educational system. Critical pedagogists look at who is left out of or denied opportunities to learn and how to create learning opportunities that are easily accessible for all.

Critical Pedagogy

A person learns as a result of opportunities provided to her/him by the society in which she/he lives. Not a learning theory but a political perspective that asks who controls learning opportunities and how are they controlled. Whose curriculum is it? When is instruction culturally-responsive? When is instruction not relevant?

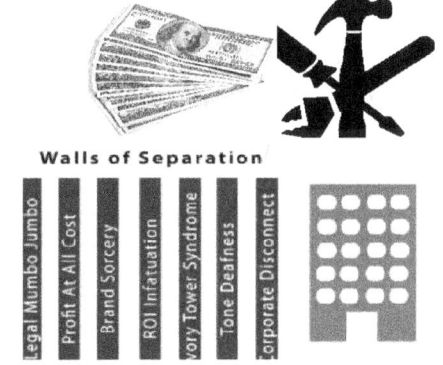

Walls of Separation

Selected theorists: Pablo Freire, Michael Apple, Ira Shor, Lisa Delpit, Peter McClaren, Rudolfo Chávez-Chávez, Shirley R. Steinberg.

Designing teaching based on types of learning

There is one last critical component to add to this short overview of the last 100 years of learning theory. This last section talks about the reason most of us want to know something about learning.

If we know how people learn we can design appropriate teaching strategies and materials. Robert Gagne was the first person who worked to connect learning to instruction. He also forever complicated the notion of learning, since he convincingly showed that there are four or five different types of learning each of which require specific kinds of instruction (his word) or teaching strategies. These different types of learning include kinesthetic learning, vocabulary and conceptual learning, problem solving, and attitudinal learning.

On the next page is a table that connects types of learning to appropriate teaching strategies. The evolution of learning and different types of learning is a fundamental consideration when developing learning design.

Learning Type & Characteristics	Teaching Strategies
Psychomotor Learning Long-lasting, like riding a Bike, once you know it is ingrained in your nervous and bodily system.	Practice, Practice, Practice Teach in steps and then put the steps together into more complete behavior.
Conceptual Learning Can be fleeting if not presented with adequate images and connections. Gagne included vocabulary as necessary to build concepts.	Group new concepts with known content, Group concepts in simple to remember systems. Add images to create visual concept maps. Example: computer systems are made up of input, processing, memory, and output.
Problem-Solving and Cognitive Strategies These are strategies for solving problems and result in long lasting learning as result of work being done by the learner.	Requires multiple experiences with problem solving and experience using cognitive strategies. May require incubation or down time during the learning process.
Attitudinal Learning How people feel about a subject. How people treat each other and work together. Moral education.	Attitudes are learned from models and from human relationships and interactions. People need to have fully developed relationships to learn attitudes.

Overview of the Chapters

The rest of the chapters in this book follow to some extent the historical evolution of learning theory - from beliefs that unconscious and inherited traits drive learning to behavioral learning theories, the cognitive movement in learning, the growth of constructivism, and finally the current emphasis on brain-based learning. In addition there are several chapters in this book in which that focus on specific applications of learning theory as chosen by the doctoral student writers.

The following chapters provide additional information on the applications of learning theories in specific contexts. There is a chapter on psychomotor learning by Nate Shaver, a doctoral student studying sport psychology. There is also a chapter on language learning by Jennifer Green, one of the editors and a graduate student in Teaching English Speakers to Other Languages (TESOL) who has taught English as a Second Language in the United States and Spain. Two graduate students, Gary Bond, who facilitates distance learning for a school district, and Brandon McIntire who works with adaptive Physical Education, worked together to contribute a chapter on the Americans with Disabilities Act and Learning Theories. Finally there is a chapter by Laura Carrillo, a doctoral student and school administrator, and Gary Bond on organizational learning, which includes information on adult learning.

After this introductory chapter, the next chapter, Chapter 2 focuses on behavioral learning theory. J.T. Knight, an attorney who is the student who unfortunately passed away a year ago, and to whom the book is dedicated, wrote the chapter on behavioral learning theory .Many school practitioners still base too many of their instructional decisions on behavioral theory, and are tied to Thorndike's advice to *practice, practice, practice*. While intensive practice is useful to build fluency in any content learning, some types of learning, such as problem solving, are not well developed using a behavioral approach to learning. Problem solving requires the existence of rich problems, as well as time to solve them.

Chapter 3, an introduction to cognitive learning theory, was developed by multiple authors including Pam Duncan, a doctoral student in our distance education program; Wanda Bulger-Tamez who runs extensive mathematics professional development across New Mexico, and; Gaspard Mucundanyi a doctoral student from Rwanda; JT Knight, Nate Shaver and the professor for this class,

12

Dr. Karin Wiburg added to the cognitive learning chapter.

Chapter 4 focuses on psychomotor learning. Nate Shaver describes how the body interacts with the mind to support learning. He describes his own theoretical model, specifically for the acquisition and retention of motor skills. This model incorporates Gagne's Model of Instructional Design and a previously developed psychomotor domain taxonomy.

Chapter 5 is a chapter on experiential learning. The authors, Mehmet Ozer, a doctoral student of learning design and technology from Turkey, and Cynthia Gomez, a school administrator and first grade teacher, begin the chapter with Dewey, the first educational theorist to describe the importance of meaningful experiences as a basis for learning. Dr. Julia Parra then added significantly to this chapter based on experiential approach to learning about STEM education. This chapter expands the interactions of body, mind and emotion into learning and adds a powerful slant to a potentially transformative way of learning.

Chapter 6 describes the movement from an individualist view of learning to the role of the learning environment in influencing learning. Piaget first suggested the notion that interactions with the environment influences individual learning. Highlighted in this chapter is the work of Vygotsky and others who expanded Piaget's perspective to include interactions with tools and other people as critical for strong learning. This chapter focuses on social constructivism and adds information on critical theory such as how Paulo Friere first introduced a political perspective on learning and education.

Chapter 7 returns to our historical evolution of learning

theories by describing more recent theories of brain-based learning that have evolved from cognitive theory. J.T. Knight and Gaspard Mucundanyi were the authors of this chapter, which points in the direction of future research for learning based on advances by science and technology to study the brain in much more depth than was possible in the last century.

Jennifer Green contributed Chapter 8 by writing about Language Learning, specifically, and the many challenges present in teaching English as a second or third language to native speakers of other languages. She focuses on teaching adults how to learn and speak a new language, and touches on the possibility of dual language bilingual programs.

In Chapter 9, applying learning theories to the Americans with Disabilities Act, Brandon McIntire and Gary Bond describe how learning theories can be used to enhance learning for students with disabilities. They include the influence of laws on the design of learning environments for students with special needs.

In Chapter 10 learning theories are applied to the learning of an organization. This chapter was written by two doctoral students who are also educational administrators, and focuses first on the nature of adult learning, and then on the concept of organizational learning.

All the members of the class wrote chapter 11 in a brainstorming session in which small groups typed their ideas during class into a shared Google document. All groups answered the question, *Why should people know about learning theory?* The professor remembered the old days when she had to first summarize student ideas on the board and later type some notes on a very old computer. Then there were the early computer and technology days when she typed into one computer attached to an

14

overhead, so her class could see the evolution of the discussion. Today, with students all having access to write in a common *Google doc* she could observe and interact with the small groups, and let the technology collect the text. Wow.

Chapter 2 - Behavioral Learning Theory

J.T. Knight

Ivan Pavlov (1849-1936) sought to study canine saliva, and found that the introduction of meat powder would induce that effect. Inadvertently, he also observed that the mere appearance of the dogs' human feeders had the same effect, even without giving the dogs any reward. Pushing his experiment further, he established that dogs could be also 'classically conditioned' to salivate on command with nothing more than the ringing of a bell. Today this is called a Pavlovian effect

Ivan Pavlov

Continuing to investigate classical conditioning, Edward Lee Thorndike (1874-1949) and other researchers studied animal behavior through the use of "puzzle-boxes" in which a confined animal would learn to escape by tapping a key or pushing a lever. After repeated efforts, the animal would escape more quickly. Thorndike observed that those behaviors that failed to release the animals (such as chewing at their cage) eventually became "extinct." Automated (learned) behaviors that released the lever so that the animal received a reward (*satisfaction*) reflected Thorndike's "law of acquired brain connections." This is why parents have learned not to reward unwanted behaviors, like temper tantrums, in kids. Eventually such behaviors should become "extinct".

Thorndike hypothesized that the educational environment presented a scenario that could provide opportunities to introduce experiments in order to produce 'better' students: "just as to make a plant grow well the gardener must act in the accordance with the laws of botany . . . so to make human beings more intelligent and useful the teacher must act in accordance with the laws of the sciences of human nature" (Thorndike, 1906, p.

Edward Thorndike

7). Thorndike's botany metaphor is apt: vegetation has been shown to be "trainable," for example, in the case of the sensitive plant, *mimosa pudica*, which can 'learn' over time to ignore being dropped, which would otherwise cause its leaves to fold (Pollan, 2013).

Thorndike's identified incentives in educational settings included the teacher's classroom attitude, as well as the physical, material, and social conditions of the particular school. The types of student responses he studied included physiological, knowledge-based, emotive and behavioral. Thorndike proposed a scientific method for testing teacher effectiveness by dividing 10-20 students of relatively equal aptitude in classes between two teachers who would each employ different instructional techniques, and then compared the results. He acknowledged the limitations of his teaching experiment in the real world of schools since so many variables were present. In later life, he tried to track success outside the school environment.

Believing that conditioned animal behaviors could be applied across species, B.F. Skinner (1904-1990) found that he was able to train pigeons to play ping-pong and peck a key for food. Like Thorndike, he argued that behavioral modification could be applied to improve the science of learning and the art of teaching (Skinner, 1954). In simple terms, he asserted that human beings are born without any intrinsic knowledge

B. F. Skinner

and accordingly have inherently plastic brains and behavior. Thus, people - regardless of social status - may be molded by the precise scientific application of rewards and punishments, into whatever the producer wants them to be. In his early view, individual preferences are unimportant, extinguishable or both. Today, with support from the field of brain research, it is clear that each of us has inherited many ways of behaving and being and that the shaping of these tendencies is usually complex.

Skinner later introduced the concept of "operant conditioning," where the operant (subject) is permitted to make a choice. The true voluntariness of the choice available in operant conditioning remains one of the major advantages of this approach over classical conditioning. Skinner reasoned that desired behavioral choices, when positively reinforced, would cause an incremental approximation in behavior toward the producer's desired outcome. Conversely, when undesired behavioral choices are met either with punishment (for example, an electric shock) or negative reinforcement (such as the deprivation of a reward), they

19

will be weakened over time. The subject's own internally driven interests-however constructed - are rendered irrelevant, and his theory remains totally opposed to the philosophical approach of John Dewey.

Positive reinforcement may be provided in ratios or intervals. Reinforcement by ratio means that the behavior might be rewarded every third time for example. Intermittent Reinforcement is supposed to lead to a longer lasting effect. Thus, unannounced, "pop"-quizzes provide a student incentive to keep up with the material they are being taught.

Skinner, like Thorndike, applied his scientific principles to education, specifically criticizing the inadequacy of the methodology of math teaching at the time:

> Few pupils ever reach the stage at which automatic reinforcements follow the natural consequences of mathematical behavior. On the contrary, the figures and symbols of mathematics have become standard emotional stimuli. The glimpse of a column of figures, not to say an algebraic symbol or integral sign, is likely to set off - not mathematical behavior - but a reaction of anxiety, guilt, or fear. (Skinner, 1999, p. 204).

To better condition students to math concepts, Skinner proposed what essentially amounts to manipulated puzzle-boxes for children, in which they can select a correct answer on a machine and the device provides some kind of reward. It was Skinner who actually created the first teaching machine in the classroom in which students could work through simple lessons, take mini-quizzes and either get a reward and move on to learning more or would be punished by going back and doing the same lesson again.

Interestingly, Skinner's ideas for mathematics puzzles and lessons are not unlike many of the digital mathematical applications that are available today. The professor for this class, Dr. Karin Wiburg used a Skinner-like teaching machine in her own middle-school mathematics class in the 1960's to learn how to use a slide rule.

By the 1980s much of behaviorism was replaced first by cognitive behavioral theory and eventually by social constructivism and cognitive science. In the 1950s, Noam Chomsky emphasized the importance of distinguishing between thought and action: "A response does not cease to be a demand if it is not followed; nor does a question become a command if the speaker answers it because of an

Noam Chomsky

implied or imagined threat" (Chomsky, 1959, p. 41). Chomsky also identified the significance of ongoing research, which showed that birds' songs were imprinted onto their embryos before they hatched. That discovery corresponds with recent revelations in humans that the diversity and complexity of vocabulary to which small children are exposed directly affects--as soon as age three--a full year's ability to understand colors, letters, numbers, sizes and shapes.

On a more fundamental level, human babies are not as malleable as Skinner imagined: research has shown their preference for human faces over other images, their ability to mimic a face directly in front of them, to distinguish colors, and to be puzzled when shown a depiction of a heavy object seemingly floating in mid-air in defiance of gravity (Roberson, Pak, & Hanley, 2008).

The contribution of behaviorism to learning theory remains important for purposes of classroom management. Through *intermittent assessments*, it can also reinforce student responsibility for the material being learned. However, teachers should be cautioned that there are limits to behaviorism beyond their control, such as students' home environment and their exposure to adverse environmental conditions before the age of three.

Delayed gratification

Several studies have examined the willpower of children to choose between accepting a treat (sometimes food, other times a toy) right away or waiting a short time for a better reward. The most famous of these experiments were conducted at Stanford University in the 1960s and involved marshmallows. Not surprisingly, children's ability to delay gratification correlated positively with the child's age. It correlated negatively with obesity (Nederkoorn, Braet, Van Eijs, Tanghe, & Jansen, 2006) and with poverty, for the reason that children in impoverished environments may wisely observe that if they wait for a reward, there will be nothing because of intense competition for that scarce resource in their home setting (Evans, 2008).

Students involved in these early experiments are still being observed as part of Stanford's research. Subsequent studies examined possible correlations between the child's choice and his or her behavioral resilience during adolescence and later in life. Preschoolers who "delayed longer" had been described by parents "as more verbally fluent," self-reliant, confident, had higher self-esteem, less ritualistic, less envious, and more resilient under stress, descriptors that only became stronger in adolescence. (Mischel & Baker, 1975.)

International comparisons have found that Chinese-Canadian and Hong Kong-based Chinese children are better able to delay reward gratification than their European-Canadian counterparts (Li, 2013). This suggests that there is a familial and or cultural component of a child's ability to wait (Tharp,1991). But even assuming a cultural difference among young children, schools are not powerless to engage in behavioral modification, at least with respect to cognitive academic performance.

So why should I know about Behavioral Theory?

It is useful to understand both classical and operant conditioning since in life we are often in situations that can be reflected by these theories. Sometimes we use the theory ourselves and other times we are in situations where one of these theories is used on us.

For example, we understand classical conditioning when we walk by a special restaurant or food store and we start salivating.

The idea of rewarding teachers based on student growth measured on standardized tests is a type of operant conditioning intended to change teacher behavior. Whether operant conditioning in this case will lead to more learning for teachers and/or students is an important question.

Finally, understanding how these theories work helps in understanding what is or is not happening.

References

Chomsky, N. (1959). A review of BF Skinner's verbal behavior. *Language, 35*(1), 26-58.

Evans, J. S. B. (2008). Dual-processing accounts of reasoning, judgment, and social cognition. *Annu. Rev. Psychol., 59*, 255-278.

Li, D. F., Lian, L., Qu, L. J., Chen, Y. M., Liu, W. B., Chen, S. R., & Yang, N. (2013). A genome-wide SNP scan reveals two loci associated with the chicken resistance to Marek's disease. *Animal genetics, 44*(2), 217-222.

Mischel, W. & Baker, N. (1975). Cognitive appraisals and transformations in delay behavior. *Journal of Personality and Social Psychology, 32*, 254-261.

Nederkoorn, C., Braet, C., Van Eijs, Y., Tanghe, A., & Jansen, A. (2006). Why obese children cannot resist food: the role of impulsivity. *Eating behaviors, 7*(4), 315-322.

Pollan, M. (2013). The intelligent plant. *New Yorker, 23*, 92-105.

Roberson, D., Pak, H., & Hanley, J. R. (2008). Categorical perception of colour in the left and right visual field is verbally mediated: Evidence from Korean. *Cognition, 107*(2), 752-762.

Skinner, B. F. (1954). The science of learning and the art of teaching. *Harvard Educational Review, 24*, 86-97.

Skinner, B. F. (1996). The science of learning and the art of teaching. In D. P. Ely, & T. Plomp, *Classic writings on instructional technology (pp. 199-210* (Vol. 1). Englewood, CO: Libraries Unlimited.

Tharp, R. G. (1991). Cultural diversity and treatment of children. *Journal of Consulting and Clinical Psychology, 59*(6), 799.

Thorndike, E. L. (1906). *The principles of teaching based on psychology.* New York, A. G. Seiler.

Additional Readings

Bodzin, A. M., Waller, P. L., Santoro, L. E., & Kale, D. (2007). Investigating the use of inquiry & web-based activities with inclusive biology learners. *The American Biology Teacher, 69*(5), 273-279.

Common Core State Standards Initiative. (2010). Common Core State Standards for Mathematics. Washington, DC: National Governors Association Center for Best Practices and the Council of Chief State School Officers.

Dewey, J. (1997). *How we think.* Courier Corporation.

Eastwell, P. (2009). Letters: Inquiry learning: Elements of confusion and frustration. *The American Biology Teacher, 71*(5), 263-266.

Gagné, R. M. (1985). *The conditions of learning and theory of instruction* (p. 304). New York: Holt, Rinehart and Winston.

Jayanti, R. K., & Singh, J. (2010). Pragmatic learning theory: An inquiry-action framework for distributed consumer learning in online communities. *Journal of Consumer Research, 36*(6), 1058-1081.

Polya, G. (1945). How to solve it: A new aspect of mathematical method. Princeton University Press.

Savery, J. R. (2006). Overview of problem-based learning: Definitions and distinctions. *Interdisciplinary Journal of Problem-based Learning, 3*(1), 9-20.

Snead, D., & Young, B. (2003). Using concept mapping to aid African American students' understanding in middle grade science. *Journal of Negro Education*, 333-343.

Tilly, W. D. (2008). The evolution of school psychology to science-based practice: Problem solving and the three-tiered model. *Best practices in school psychology V, 1*, 17-36

Trombulak, S. C. (1995). Merging inquiry-based learning with near-peer teaching. *BioScience*, 412-416.

Wertheimer, M. (1959). *Productive thinking.* New York: Harper & Row.

Wragg, T. (2004). An Icon of the Mind, *Times Education Supplement: London*, No. 4595.

Chapter 3 - Cognitive Learning Theory

Nathaniel Shaver, Karin Wiburg, Gaspard Mucundanyi, Wanda

Bulger-Tamez, J.T. Knight

In order to understand the significance of cognitive learning theory, one must learn first about how the original theory of cognitive learning occurred. Psychologists began to question the traditional behavioral theory of the early 20th century. Ivan Pavlov and his lesser known colleague, Ivan Fillipovitch Tolochinov, conducted classical conditioning research that attributed learning to the association of an unconditioned stimulus that invokes a particular response with a novel stimulus (Pavlov, 1927). Pavlov and his dogs were described in the previous chapter on behaviorism. These experiments demonstrated that behavior could be invoked or 'learned' via the conditioned associations created by each stimulus. J.B. Watson, an originator of behaviorism theory of the late 19th and early 20th centuries, did not believe it was useful to study the conscious mind and instead considered behavior to be the most useful measure of human action. B.F. Skinner, one of Watson's students, was also convinced that behavior and its environmental influences propelled learning. Within Skinner's analysis, Behavioral 'theory' used previous behavior from a stimulus to account for an action that may occur (Skinner, 1950).

However, psychology theorists began to question the *source* of behavior, bringing the mind to light. Behaviorism did not take into account the minds' expansive networking and the mental processes

that take place between the stimuli being presented and the

responses being produced. Skinner's concept of operant conditioning demonstrated the effect of reinforcement & punishment, but disregarded consciousness and perception. Cognitive psychology developed as a result of questioning the *origination* of behavior.

Objective deductive research also reinforced the capabilities of cognition to support latent learning. Even before Skinner, Edward C. Tolman studied rats and their learning of directionality within a maze. He found that rats placed within a maze structure without food quickly navigated to the food once

Edward C. Tolman

they were exposed to it within the maze. Within a single day they even became as efficient as the ones who were continuously provided food and whose behavior was continuously reinforced (Tolman, 1948). This very early experiment supported the idea that learning does not always result from direct reinforcement. Further research conducted by Tolman continued to support the cognitive capabilities of the mind (Tolman, 1948).

Another revolutionary psychologist, Noam Chomsky, opposed Skinner's view of language as being learned through operant conditioning. Chomsky conducted research that supported the theory that words were spontaneously generated even if they were not rewarded (Chomsky, 1959). He also noticed that children have the mental capacity to naturally understand the rules of language and have an awareness of how most words are converted into the past tense by adding *ed*, (e.g. walked, talked, and stopped). Young children generalize this rule, for example, by using the word *swimmed* as the past tense of swim and *fighted* as the past tense of fight. This is a sign of progress, not a mistake, and shows the ability of the children to express themselves by naturally using common rules of language and applying them to new words. Chomsky believed that this process was built into the mind from birth as a sort of language acquisition device, which operated without external reinforcement.

M.C. Wittrock, a major educational psychologist, wrote a pivotal paper called the *Cognitive Movement in Instruction* (Wittrock, 1978) and was foundational in connecting new findings in psychology to the purpose of this learning theory for instruction. In this popular paper, which followed an invited lecture at the

M.C. Wittrock

1978 American Educational Research Conference (AERA), Wittrock's first words reflected the move from behavioral to cognitive psychology. His introduction to this paper begins, "It has often been said that psychology lost its soul a long time ago, destroyed its mind at the turn of the 20th century, and now is having trouble with its behavior" (Wittrock, 1978,p. 15). He answered his own introduction by saying that the mind is still very much alive and processing information. He went on to suggest that in the 1970s a cognitive approach to learning meant that it was scientifically more productive to study the internal processing of the learner than the effect of the environment on learning.

Wittrock went on to suggest that it was important for those interested in improving teaching and learning to study learning as an internal cognitively-mediated process rather than the result of the environment, or a reinforcement by other people. He suggested, for

29

example, that someone interested in studying how teaching styles influence learning should note internally-driven behaviors of the learner such as paying attention, processing ideas in different ways, and using imagery or several interpretations of the content, to improve the strength of learning.

By this point most educational psychologists and instructional designers began to configure ways to enhance learning by engaging the learner in opportunities to interact with and think about the content being studied. In the 1980s there was a strong move to support student-initiated problem-solving, inquiry-based methods, and reciprocal teaching (Brown & Campione, 1994), a process of helping students make sense of text by rephrasing what they read in their own words.

Another well-known learning theorist, Richard Mayer (1992) wrote about the historic meeting of cognition and instruction that evolved during the 1980s. In this article, Mayer examined the emergence of cognitive approaches to instruction with hope that an understanding of the origins of this field will yield perspective on where it is going. He presents a historical analysis of the relationship between psychology and education, especially cognitive psychology and instruction. He then suggests a historical evolution of learning based on three views of learning and instruction: learning as response acquisition, learning as knowledge acquisition, and learning as knowledge construction. Each of these views of learning is described in more detail with a focus on the cognitive processes.

The 1980s was a promising period for educational research and learning psychology as a curriculum was designed in most content areas to focus on helping students make sense of what they were learning. Mathematics and science instruction were a natural environment for designing cognitively-guided learning opportunities. Providing time for teachers to question, and students to explore, became a natural part of quality teaching. However, if there was an academic weakness during this time, it might have been a lack of quality professional learning for current and future teachers. To practice cognitively-guided instruction, it was necessary for teachers to become experts in both the content area and the pedagogical system for teaching it.

With this new conception of learning, *learners are once again responsible for and accountable for their own learning.* Wittrock and other cognitive theorists suggested that cognitive learning theory goes back to the early Greeks and was first seen in Socrates use of asking questions to facilitate learning. An example of Socratic inquiry is presented below. A second example is the use of learner problem solving, which is facilitated by the teacher's use of inquiry. Using these cognitive approaches to instruction requires that a teacher knows the content well and knows how to set up interesting and meaningful problems for students. The teacher must also know how to ask progressively more complex questions that lead students to higher levels of thinking and experimentation.

Inquiry-Based Learning

One type of cognitive constructivist, experience-based, learning is inquiry-based learning (IL), often linked to problem-based learning (PBL). The American Association for the Advancement of Science has identified the goal of IL as "to make all students scientifically literate, able to apply scientific knowledge to improve their own lives, deal with an increasingly technological world and make science-related decisions as responsible citizens" (as cited in Niess, 2016, p. 55). Its origins are as ancient and as diverse as Confucius and Socrates.

PBL originated in medical schools in the 1960s as a method to actively involve student interns in the diagnosis and treatment of patients to achieve a particular learning outcome as designated by the teacher and the curriculum. PBL is distinct from case-based learning used in psychology or law where a set of facts is provided but no particular outcome is required. IL is frequently used in the sciences, particularly in posing hypotheses, structuring research, and critically evaluating data. Both methods support student-centered learning, and reject the rote memorization and unanalyzed regurgitation of curricular content and factual knowledge. A process which Freire called, "banking education".

One of the benefits of IL is that it is student-driven, but instructor-controlled. IL is not unguided, as some critics have asserted; rather, teachers provide the lesson framework and often the original data sources that can be used to address an issue (or at least guidance on how to find useful resources). Students are invited to ask, answer, and communicate their own questions even though they may have an incomplete *schema* about a particular topic. In doing so, students are free to make mistakes in a safe, collaborative environment, realize what they already know and what they need to learn, and gradually learn which guiding questions will help them to progress in their inquiry. Through repetition of inquiry and time for problem solving, students build confidence and critical thinking skills, including identifying whether they have complete information, whether the source of their information is credible, and whether an argument is based on data or opinion. Accordingly, students become better able to draw logical conclusions, and identify how certain conditions may predictably change results. Since IL typically requires students to acquire a new and unfamiliar skill set in approaching learning, *scaffolding* can help reduce the cognitive load students experience from having to learn new material in a new way. Teachers can join with the students in learning content more deeply during an inquiry. By cooperatively distributing learning expectations, students are reassured that their participation is essential to a specific lesson. Because students in the IL context assume responsibility for their own learning, they are more engaged with the material. Students taught under the IL method retain the knowledge and procedures they have learned and are better able to apply it across subject and disciplines. They also begin to ask their own essential questions. As the phrase attributed to Confucius goes, "Tell me and I forget; teach me and I may remember; involve me and I will learn".

A Specific Example of Inquiry Learning: The Socratic Method in Legal Education

Typically, the Socratic classroom method puts individual students on the spot to determine why one result does, and indeed should, differ from another. Court cases and legal doctrines with dissimilar results are juxtaposed so as to invite students themselves to resolve differing judicial outcomes. Anyone who has seen "Judge Judy" has been exposed to Socratic adversarial questioning and can usually recognize when participants are being guided (by the court) against their own interest.

In a Socratic classroom, there are active and passive participants. Active students are called upon "blindly," or randomly, by the professor, while passive students participate vicariously. One can imagine student-prompted words such as "unfair", "wrong", "immoral", "unconstitutional", slowly being placed on what will become the perimeter of a chalkboard circle: a physical manifestation of circular reasoning, wherein students (however active) are not yet dealing with the merits of an underlying policy debate, or conflict among policy goals.

The Socratic method has been criticized as being too harsh, ritualistic and not unlike hazing. Jerome Bruner, building on Piaget as a foundation, notes that lawyers with better linguistic skills use words to further marginalize the less fortunate. Of course, this is not a Socratic goal, merely a byproduct of a misuse of the method. Put another way, what may be "wordplay" for one party, may be torture for another. Any unprepared law student knows the feeling all too well. It should be noted that law schools are moving away from the Socratic-only model and have been for some time.

A related method, the teaching of problem solving is presented in the next section. It describes the problem-solving method using examples from the mathematics classroom.

Problem Solving

On a daily basis, people solve problems at work and home. The problem solving process is cognitive and is often facilitated by the previous knowledge that is stored in a learner's long-term memory that aids in understanding and analyzing a problem. A person uses a combination of learned knowledge and new planning to discover a strategy that provides the optimum solution. Hence, problem solving "yields new learning" (Gagne, 1985, p. 178). Problem solving is greatly used in mathematics, medicine, engineering, artificial intelligence and computer science although it can also be useful in all content areas and can improve retention of knowledge in all academic areas. Problem solving can also be used as part of our daily activities.

In 1971, George Polya wrote, *"A teacher of mathematics has a great opportunity. If he [she] fills the allotted time [for teaching] with drilling students in routine problems he kills their interest, hampers their intellectual development, and misuses his opportunity. But if he challenges the curiosity of students by setting them problems proportionate to their knowledge, and helps them to solve their problems with stimulating questions, he may give them a taste for, and some means of, independent thinking."(p. v)*

One of the fathers of a famous method for mathematical problem solving is George Polya (1887-1985), a Hungarian mathematician who taught mathematics in Zurich, Switzerland and later immigrated to the United States to teach at Stanford. Polya devised a problem solving process to support students in developing problem solving skills. He believed that problem solving abilities were not innate, but represented a thinking process that can be taught and learned (Polya, 1945).

Polya outlines a four phase plan for problem solving: (1) Understand the problem to see clearly what is required, (2) devise a plan by analyzing how the various items of the problem are connected and how the solution we are looking for is related to the given data, (3) carry out the plan, and (4) look back to reflect on and reexamine the result as well as the plan that led to your solution. By engaging in this process frequently students can consolidate their knowledge and develop their ability to problems solve (Polya, 1945). Of course it is necessary for students to be given the opportunity to solve a lot of problems in the classroom in order for students to develop this skill.

Focusing on problem solving in education, many researchers like Gagne (1985), emphasize the importance of supporting the learner's capabilities in problem solving through three types of knowledge:

i.   Intellectual skills which are rules, principles, and concepts required to solve the problem.
ii.   Organized verbal information (concepts) which is needed for a learner to understand the problem, and
iii. Cognitive strategies that involve the selection of appropriate knowledge and skills and decisions of making them and how to apply them in order to reach on solution. (Gagne, 1985, p. 188).

Even though many researchers have worked to understand problem solving, only a few have tried to provide information about the process that occurs in the brain when solving problems. Dewey (1910) wrote about the sequence of problem solving as having five steps. (1) Presentation of the problem, (2) definition of the problem, (3) formulate hypothesis, (4) verify the hypothesis or (5) formulate a new hypothesis until the learner has achieved an adequate solution. Gagne (1985) points out that all except the first of these steps to problem solving are internal cognitive processes. By enacting these internal processes, learners develop cognitive strategies that govern thinking behavior. Engaging in problem solving is a cognitive exercise that develops learners' ability to apply thinking rules. These rules become part of a repertoire of higher-order thinking strategies accessible to the learner. As mentioned earlier in Chapter 1, cognitive strategies, tend to be sustained once learned and can be remembered and used in future learning.

Implications of Problem-solving in Mathematics Education

Problem-solving methods are connected to the Standards for Mathematical Practice in the Common Core State Standards for Mathematics or more commonly written, CCSS-M (National Governors Association Center for Best Practices, Council of Chief State School Officers, 2010). The CCSS-M, which has been adopted in most states, calls for the students to "make sense of problems and persevere in problem solving." According to CCSS-M, students at all grade levels should learn to explain the meaning of a problem and look for an entry point to its solution. The students plan a solution pathway by analyzing constraints and relationships rather than quickly jumping into a solution attempt. They may try simpler forms of the original problem to gain insight into their solution strategy and should monitor and evaluate their progress in using this strategy and change course if necessary. Students should check their answers to problems using a different method, and they should continually ask themselves, "Does this make sense?"
(http://www.corestandards.org/Math/Practice/)

Developing problem-solving skills is about developing students' thinking abilities around choosing appropriate strategies for different kinds of problems. This learning takes longer than memorizing a set of rules or procedures, but because it develops long-term semantic meaning the learning is more likely to be retrievable in the future. The time spent on problem solving is more beneficial to future learning than only memorizing rules. Problem-solving ability means students have the reproductive thinking skills to use their current knowledge to solve similar problems as well as novel and different problems in the future.

Technology metaphors for problem solving and thinking.

37

With the growth in computer technology from the 1970s to the 1990's there was an increase in attempts to explain thinking and problem solving by comparing the brain to the work of the computer. With the emergence of computer processing, Newell (1980), Gagne (1985), and other cognitive learning theorists began to consider how problem-solving processing might relate to computer processing. Perhaps thinking of the brain as something like a computer can help humans understand problem solving better. Here are 5 examples of this kind of thinking:

1. **Big switch**: The problem solver has a large number of learned procedures and has a big switch to access and find the specific procedures that can be used to solve a specific problem. For example: A computer has many files and folders and it has switches to identify the required file or to call up the correct software sequence.

2. **Big memory**: The problem solver has multiple sets of organized information in memory that allows her or him to access many ideas which are helpful in solving the problem. For example: A computer saves files and folder on a hard disk and tries to organize those folders within larger concepts or groups of ideas.

3. **Weak method**: The problem solvers use cognitive strategies which are overly generalized and do not provide a support for solving specific problems. This is a common strategy used by beginners in trying to solve problems.
   Example: When searching for a file, the computer brings up too many files from which to choose. The result is a lack of specific ideas for a solution.

4. **Mapping**: The problem is mapped to something known so the problem can be solved using a known method.
   Example: When we are looking for a file, a computer takes the

name of the file and compares it to every file saved in memory in order to find a match.

5. **Planning**: The problem solver develops a plan which helps her/him to solve the problem. Example: The processor (brain of the computer) executes the search request of searching a file and provides the name of a file or indicates that the file is not available.

The Current State of Cognitive Learning Theory

We are not sure what happened in education that resulted in a refocus on testing and the learning of small units of behavior to meet discrete course objectives. This focus on learning reflects traditional behavioral theory. One reason might be that there has been a national concern that students in the United States were scoring lower in mathematics and literacy than many other nations as measured on international tests such as the TIMMS, and PISA. The reaction to this current problem was not like the earlier reaction by the U.S. leaders to the launching of the Russian satellite Sputnik, which at that time facilitated a growth of programs to increase deep learning of science and mathematics through problem solving and inquiry. This involved the use of a cognitive-based learning theory. Currently, perhaps because of the political climate in the 1990s, political leaders called for an external control of teachers and students and frequent testing as a way to speed up achievement and catch up to students' performances in other countries. The *No Child Left Behind Act* in the United States was legislated to gain better control over who was teaching and learning math, reading, and literacy. The one good outcome of this legislation was that it became obvious through the collected data that many ethnically diverse and low-income students were scoring much lower on these

39

tests than mainstream white students. These findings could be used to support a movement for equity. However, in general this legislation did nothing to reform how the students were being taught and how teachers need to be well educated for students to become well educated, a strategy adopted in in the 21st century in Finland to improve educational outcomes.

More recently the Common Core movement suggested standards for learning so that all students in different states would have the opportunity to be taught using higher learning standards. However, this initial movement for deeper and more specific goals became a testing movement in which much of the school day has become preparation for the test, rather than opportunities for deep learning. In addition teachers are being judged by their students' performance on standardized tests. How these tests were developed and what they are really testing is currently an intense educational debate. Despite the political movement to test and control teachers, educational leaders and researchers continue to believe in the cognitive movement in instruction, which has continued to grow with support from extensive research.

On Sunday, May 17th, 2015 the New York Times printed an opinion/editorial by David Kohn that included evidence that children learn more from play in the early grades than from being drilled in mathematics or reading exercises and using worksheets. Kohn (2015) started the article by recalling the days 20 years ago when children played with blocks, drew and created imaginary worlds in their heads and with their classmates. He mentioned that play has been replaced with didactic teaching in a style used in higher grade levels. Fears are spread nationwide that if children do not receive instruction in phonics and math facts in earlier grades they will never catch up. However, a growing number of scientists and educational researchers say there is little evidence to support this approach, and in fact, these strategies may hinder learning and even reduce achievement.

He describes a trend that expert Nancy Carlsson-Paige, a professor at Lesley University in Cambridge, Massachusetts, describes as a "profound misunderstanding of how children learn." Carlsson-Paige explains that she visits schools and sees that children are forced to just sit at a table and copy letters.

In fact, in Finland and in Estonia, children do not start formal education until age 7 and the scores in the latest international test, the Program for International Student Assessment (PISA) for student performance are significantly higher than U.S. scores in math, science, and reading. The PISA, unlike some earlier tests, provides opportunities for students to demonstrate their thinking and problem-solving abilities.

Jay Giedd, a neuroscientist at the University of California at San Diego has spent his career studying how the human brain develops from birth through adolescence and says most kids younger than seven or eight are better suited to learning through active exploration rather than receiving didactic instruction. Reading, in particular, cannot be rushed because of the nature of the developing brain. Many boys, in particular, may need an extra year to learn reading and if formal reading instruction is not required of them, they might spontaneously read well by age eight.

Finally, with the advancements in neuropsychology and an increased ability of scientists to study how the brain actually works, cognitive psychology has been developed to integrate current brain-based learning (see Chapter 7). In fact, none other than M.C.

Wittrock (2013), the author of the cognitive movement in instruction, recently published an edited book entitled, *The Brain and Psychology*. He uses this book to describe how research on neuroscience and research on the cognitive learning processes have had very divergent views of learning, but it might be time to bring them together. Eventually, new research on brain-based learning can help to relate the brain's activities to theories of cognitive processing.

Why should I learn about cognitive learning theory?

How a person perceives and thinks about a subject has a major effect on how that subject is learned. Students may have different backgrounds and very different ways of looking at any subject. Finding out how students perceive and process information is essential to providing learning opportunities that make sense to students.

A very simple experiment to try to see the differences in the neuron networks in each student's brain is the following:

Tell students you are thinking of a word, for example, DOG, and then ask them to think of the next word they think of after DOG , and then another word and then another and to remember the last word they thought of. It is amazing how every person will have a different word and how different those words will be.

Do not assume that we all think alike.

References

Brown, A. L., & Campione, J. C. (1994). *Guided discovery in a community of learners*. The MIT Press.

Chomsky, N. (1959). A review of BF Skinner's verbal behavior. *Language, 35*(1), 26-58.

Gagné, R. M. (1985). *The conditions of learning and theory of instruction*. New York: Holt, Rinehart and Winston.

Kohn, D. (2015, May 17). Let the kids learn through play. *The New York Times.*

Mayer, R. E. (1992). Cognition and instruction: Their historic meeting within educational psychology. *Journal of Educational Psychology, 84*(4), 405-412.

Niess, M. (Ed.). (2016). *Handbook of research on transforming mathematics teacher education in the digital age*. IGI Global.

Pavlov, I. P. (1927). *Conditional reflexes: An investigation of the physiological activity of the cerebral cortex*. H. Milford.

Polya, G (1971). *How to solve it.* New York: Doubleday Anchor.

Polya, G. (1945). *How to solve it: A new aspect of mathematical method.* Princeton University Press

Skinner, B. F. (1950). Are theories of learning necessary?. *Psychological Review, 57*(4), 193-216.

Tolman, E. C. (1948). Cognitive maps in rats and men. *Psychological Review, 55*(4), 189

Wittrock, M. C. (1978). The cognitive movement in instruction. *Educational Psychologist, 13*(1), 15-29.

Wittrock, M. C. (Ed.). (2013). *The brain and psychology*. Academic Press.

Chapter 4- Psychomotor Learning

Nathaniel Shaver

The Psychomotor Domain

Elizabeth Jane Simpson understood the need to elaborate on psychomotor teaching and learning because nearly all professions, and even daily tasks, involve high-level motor control in continuity with mind and body functions. She developed and tested a classification system, which was directed towards the difficulty of each task, sequencing learning experiences and the skill level required in carrying out each motor activity (Simpson, 1970).

Her first reference to the psychomotor domain was in 1966 when she published *The Classification of Educational Objectives, Psychomotor Domain*. At the time, she was a professor and chair of the department of Home Economics within the College of Education at the University of Illinois. Her structural model emphasized the learning of targeted skills and the acknowledgment of a multi-modal approach. She first identified disciplines in which specific skills were essential, including Industrial Arts, Agriculture, Home Economics, Music, Physical Education and Art. Her holistic approach to learning contemplated the interaction between the mind and the body in refining a baseline ability into a particularized skill. Her theory further emphasized maximizing the efficiency of the learning environment and each individual learner's progression.

Later, as a research associate, she continued to develop, assess and implement instructional materials. Simpson's position in the U.S. Office of Education allowed her to more thoroughly develop her model. Specifically, her taxonomy was comprised of seven levels: Perception, Set, Guided Response, Mechanism, Complex Overt Response, Adaptation and Origination (Simpson, 1970).

"Perception" addresses the ability to use sensory cues to guide physical responses. These include taste, touch, smell, sight, sound and kinesthetic. "Set" includes the readiness to react, which is primarily an awareness stage or a preparatory behavior. "Guided Response" through imitation is third, while "Mechanism" is the ability to perform a skilled movement as a learned, habitual response. "Complex Overt Response" entails the ability to perform the motor act as a complex movement pattern, minimizing unnecessary movement, for smoothness and efficiency in a timely manner. This level is divided into two subcategories: resolution of uncertainty (limited mental mapping) and automatic performance (muscle control) (Simpson, 1970). "Adaptation" includes modifying the skill to fit new situations, and finally, "Origination" is the idea of an "ability to develop an original skill that replaces the skill as initially learned" (Simpson, 1970).

Previously, foundational classifications had been derived from Benjamin Bloom's 1956 *Taxonomy of Educational Objectives*, which focused educational goals on the recognition of knowledge and development of intellectual abilities and skills (Simpson, 1970). Bloom's 5-tiered cognitive plan, along with the criteria for an "affective" plan (interests, desires, appreciations and attitudes) encompassed the mastery of behavior and learning abilities. Notably absent from Bloom's taxonomy were hierarchal educational objective goals and concomitant prioritizing of psychomotor tasks.

The significance of the psychomotor domain transcends the acquisition phase of motor learning. There may be avenues directed towards cognition and affective processing *through* motor learning as a pathway itself. The influence of the actual "doing" of a task on the cognitive performance can impact the learning process itself (Abedi & O'Neil, 2005). Physical activities that support a cognitive or affective function should be labeled physical (haptic, tactile, kinesthetic) (Wilson, 2003), while the term psychomotor should be reserved for skills that have specific interpretive, physical or reflexive objectives. An example of using physical movement as a pathway for cognitive growth is using a microscope to analyze actual tissue samples, followed by drawing what is seen under the microscope. The intent is to identify and recognize the structure of the sample, but the pathway to learning cell structure may be accelerated through the physical task of drawing (Wilson, 2003).

Models relative to the psychomotor learning theory merit discussion provides a conceptual model of human performance, which includes the processes that occur and the stages of motor learning (Schmidt & Lee, 2014). Motor learning takes place in a sequential fashion, with both looped and un-looped information processing taking place through multimodal perception. Change in task performance and segmental motor skill function is dependent upon environmental conditions, exposure to prior stimuli, internal mechanisms and feedback. Motor learning begins with an input (stimulus detection).

Movement patterns can be manipulated and practiced, preprogramming the movement for rapid execution (Kawato, Furukawa & Suzuki, 1987). The psychomotor learning model provides structure directed towards learning physical skills through the manipulation of individual movements, with the goal of programming efficient movement patterns leading to automaticity General Motor Program theory (GMP) (Schmidt, 1975.) argues that movement programs can be generalized. Although a given GMP has an invariable imprint of *relative* timing and type of movement, the GMP can be adjusted by making changes to variable surface features (time, amplitude, direction, force and the limbs and muscles used to produce the action). Multiple lines of evidence support GMP theory, including reaction time and movement complexity (Henry & Rogers, 1960), Deafferentation Experiments (Blouin, Gauthier, Vercher, & Cole, 1996;Taub, 1976; Taub & Berman, 1968). Inhibiting Actions (Slater-Hammel, 1960), and Electromyography (EMG) studies (Belen'kii, Gurfinkel, & Pal'tsev, 1967).

Exteroception in the form of visual or audio information provides information about the body in relation to the environment (Schmidt & Lee, 2014). A stimulus is identified, followed by a chosen response and selected program of movement (Schmidt & Lee, 2014). This form of closed-loop processing is conscious, voluntary and controlled. Through repeated exposure to stimuli and the production of actions, *schemas* are developed. The schema is the theoretical structure that supplies the needed parameters for the movement (Schmidt & Lee, 2014). The movement pattern related to those perceptual cues will then be linked to future interactions and the specific *schema*. Because the brain simply does not have the physical capacity to create and store brand new movements every time a *similar* movement is required to be performed, it must combine programs and adapt by changing "surface" features. If a surface feature parameter of the schema within a GMP is changed, a novel action can be produced (Schmidt & Lee, 2014). As the movement pattern is executed, information is relayed through the spinal cord to the target muscles, producing the actual movement (Schmidt & Lee, 2014). During the movement *proprioception*

48

distinguishes bodily movement of joints & muscles through the vestibular apparatus, joint receptors, muscle spindles, golgi tendon organs and cutaneous receptors.

Ultimately, these receptor systems provide information needed to make necessary corrective movements (Schmidt & Lee, 2014). Within each stage, processing is taking place, whether it is automatic or manual, while loops anticipate feedback. If the learner has been exposed to the stimulus prior to the current instance, a comparator is triggered, outcome is anticipated and error is generated correlating with the movement pattern (Schmidt & Lee, 2014). The stimulus is then identified again, and the process repeats. Feedback also occurs at the level of unconscious automaticity of the monosynaptic loop (M1 loop) reflex and at the multi-synaptic (M2) reflexive loop (Schmidt & Lee, 2014). Both loops initiate an unconscious automatic response that propagates rapid changes in movement patterns.

As with Simpson (1966 and 1970), R.H. Dave (1967), and A.J. Harrow (1972) are considered to be originators within the psychomotor domain (Huitt, 2003; Driscoll, 2005). Harrow elaborated on Bloom's taxonomy while Dave had studied under Bloom. There are variations within the taxonomies of each of these pioneers.

Dave's taxonomy included 5 levels; Imitate, Manipulate, Precision, Articulation and Naturalization (Dave, 1967). "Imitate" was the observation of a skill and an attempt to repeat it. "Manipulate" involved performing the skill to produce the recognizable movement. "Precision" was the independent performance of the skill, with the goal of accuracy, proportion and exactness leading to automaticity. "Articulation" modified the skill to meet new situations and combining multiple skills in harmony. The final "Naturalization" level is the pursued perfection of combining two or more skills, with the goal of automaticity and efficiency. Interestingly, Dave's taxonomy did *not* include perception, which is necessary for stimulus detection, response selection and movement programming. In addition, it could be argued that the Naturalization is precedent to Articulation because combining skills must be completed before the combined movement pattern is perfected. Even so, Dave's observations correlate readily with Simpson's.

Harrow (1972). presents a six-category psychomotor domain which addresses the ability of the performer, skill difficulty and communication avenues; "Reflex Movements", Basic Fundamental Movements", "Perceptual Abilities", "Skilled Movements", and "Non-discursive Communication" "Reflex Movements" include reflexes which are either M1 (short latency) or M2 (long latency) and can be present at birth or emerge later through maturation. "Basic-Fundamental Movements" identify the type of movement as locomotor, non-locomotor or manipulative. These movements include walking, running, jumping, pushing, pulling, grasping and manipulating objects. They can be combined to produce elaborate sequences and complex actions. "Perceptual Abilities" defines the type of perception mode(s) used in stimulus identification.

Harrow's objectives address the further enhancement of reaction capabilities, including kinesthetic, visual, auditory, haptic (touch/tactile), and coordination. Objective "physical abilities" take into account the individuals' biological structure: their endurance, agility, flexibility, strength and mechanisms for carrying out reaction (body and specifically dexterity). Skilled movements account for the complexity of the movement pattern required to perform the desired precise movement. Skilled movements may also combine other movement types (basic fundamental

50

movements, perceptual, physical activities) that must be learned in order to perform at a very high level of efficiency and precision. Examples include hitting a baseball or softball, shooting a basketball, throwing, bowling, dancing, acting, etc. Non-discursive communication incorporates body language and expression through posture, gestures and facial expressions, all of which apply to the fine arts.

On an auditory level, in order for verbal information to trigger meaningful responses, individual taxonomy of each stage includes words to use during instruction that correspond to each individual phase of the learning.

Application

Skill acquisition and retention is the primary goal of psychomotor domain learning theory. These skills can range from gross motor skills, which are for instance, moving body segments (arms and legs - walking) to fine motor skills, digital movement of the fingers (each finger – playing the piano). In general, structuring learning plans to account for multimodal perceptual learning is essential in order to maximize the efficiency of the learning environment. The theory argues that the curricula of a given program be structured to address societal needs while preparing students with technical skills through classroom-based or industry-based experiences (Laguador & Ramos, 2014.) Specific to each discipline, each individual learning objective can be enhanced by utilizing the physical *doing* of actions in order to strengthen performance and retention of the target skill. The applications are fairly limitless, but the challenge is to distinguish when, where and how to implement (see Table 1) while considering the factors of time, setting, nature of objectives, content, available resources, institutional constraints, number of learners, individual differences and preferences (Khadjooi, Rostami & Ishaq, 2011).

Gagne's model of instructional design corresponds with this type of lesson planning. The outcomes to be achieved within the design may include verbal information, intellectual skills, cognitive strategies, attitudes, and motor skills (Gagne, Briggs & Wager, 1992). The teacher identifies specific objectives and outcomes, classifies the target type of movement(s) and then organizes the lesson. "Events of Instruction" include: 1. Gaining students' attention. 2. Informing the learner of the objective. 3. Stimulating recall of prerequisite learning. 4. Presenting the stimulus material. 5. Providing learning guidance. 6. Eliciting the performance. 7. Providing feedback. 8. Assessing the performance. 9. Enhancing retention and transfer. Additionally, 2 more events and 4 stages were created to connect the psychomotor domain to the model of instructional design. Events: "Promoting Automaticity" and "Exploratory Creativity". Stages: "Objectivity", "Presentation", "Practice", and "Feedback".

As illustrated in The Instructional Design of Psychomotor Learning (Table 1), although physical movement does not take place until stage five, prior stages prepare the response of a motor program in order to perform the most efficient and skillful movement. Stages six and seven focus on performing the skill through practice and feedback, while eight through eleven promote manipulation, automaticity, retention and exploration. To acquire specific skills, combining stages may benefit the learning atmosphere while targeting multiple stages through one objective. In addition, while there may be overlap of the affective and cognitive domains, the primary goal is motor skill influence. Considered to be one of the most valid theories of skill acquisition, Fitts and Posner also theorized stages of learning which correlate to Table 1. These stages of learning include Verbal-Cognitive, Fixation, and Autonomous (Fitts & Posner, 1967).

Chemistry (Chee & Tan, 2012), nursing (Vincent, Sheriff & Mellott, 2015; Edgecome et al., 2013), dentistry (Feil, 1992; Urbankova, 2015), and surgical procedures (McSparron et al., 2015; Verdaasdonk,Stassen, Van Wijk, & Dankelman, 2007) are just a few of the disciplines that engage physical tasks continuously throughout the instructive process. Active participation by students in any preparatory field necessitates learning by doing.

Athletics and other human performance require precision oriented movements that strive for proficiency and efficiency. Athletes use perception to select a response, produce a movement, and alter that movement for precision and kinetic sequencing of the body. Learning, manipulating and performing movement patterns drives athletic performance. Therefore, a model that takes into account every distinguishable aspect of learning is essential for productive coaching and teaching methodology.

An example of athletic skilled movement is sequencing a hitter to promote kinetic efficiency. Hitting is a considered to be one of the most difficult skills to perform consistently in order to transfer energy from the body to the bat, and to the baseball while maintaining control, power, quickness, and tempo. Utilizing previous psychomotor learning taxonomy, as well as developing specific taxonomy related to the action of hitting, psychomotor learning theory could be applied extremely and effectively when teaching how to effectively hit a baseball. Softball, golf, tennis, cricket and other sports in which manipulating an object in order to impact another object could have relatively similar taxonomies that result in effective learning of each particular skill.

Teaching effectively involves utilizing three primary domains:

cognitive, affective and psychomotor. Teachers may best target the psychomotor domain by structuring a lesson plan to include preparation for practice, actual practice, and post-practice reflection. Effective teaching in the psychomotor domain does not simply occur by lecturing, having the student "go for it" and expecting the skill to be mastered and retained. Rather, the plan should be systematically structured to effectively communicate the goals, enhance the learning process, target retention and transfer, and promote further exploration of the movement pattern in order to create new forms of skills and enhance motor programs.

TABLE 1

*A synthesized model combining Gagne's Model of Instructional Design, Psychomotor Learning Theory (Simpson, Harrow and Dave), expanded Motor Activity Significance, expanded Key Words & the added design for Events, Stage, Instructional Goals, & Implementation.

#	Event	Stage	Description	Motor Activity Significance	Key Words	Instructional Goals & Implementation
1	Gaining Attention	Perception	Essential first step in performing a motor act when the student becomes aware of the objects, qualities, or relations via sensory cues to guide motor activity.	Taking initiative to capture the attention of the students. Using an abrupt stimulus change to invoke meaningful perception is the first stage in learning.	describes, detects, differentiates, distinguishes, identifies, isolates, relates, selects	1. Starting a lesson with a thought provoking question that utilizes multiple modalities, such as audition and vision. 2. Promote the recognition of factors that are involved in properly executed/efficient movements.
2	Informing the Learner of the Objective	Objectivity	May inform the student which mechanisms will be targeted for anticipatory preparation of movement generation.	A direct statement that initiates the internal process of expectancy which may motivate the learner.	objective, complete, prepare, understand, master, perform, articulate	1. Stating the objective(s); "Upon completing this lesson you will be able to....". 2. Providing a video of a properly executed fundamental that will be learned in the lesson. 3. Providing a video of an exceptional performance, which pertains to the lesson.
3	Stimulating Recall of Prerequisite Learning	Set	May initiate thought processes that trigger the visual and kinaesthetic representations of skills that were learned prior, especially if sequence is imperative.	The readiness to act which includes mental, physical, and emotional sets regarding disposition that determines the student's willingness to engage. (Passive or Participatory, Body Positioning & Focus of Receptors, Disposition & Desire).	begins, displays, explains, moves, proceeds, reacts, shows, states, volunteers	1. Recognizing abilities and limitations. 2. Recalling previously learned skills, which may be applied to novel situations. 3. Promoting readiness to respond to instruction by limiting distraction.
4	Presenting the Stimulus Material	Presentation	Multimodal perception of new skills.	New skills are thoroughly explained, demonstrated and broken down into meaningful steps.	meaning, feel, achieve, see, watch, listen, view, interact, analyze, debrief	1. The skill to be learned is presented via video. 2. The skill to be learned is presented via live demonstration. 3. The skill to be learned is presented verbally and via text.
5	Providing Learning Guidance	Guided Response	The early practice stages in learning a complex skill that includes imitation and trial and error.	Defining the requirements for task performance and measuring them via objective practice results that are executed by the performer.	copies, traces, follows, react, reproduce, responds, rationale, logic, reason, imitation	1. The skill is emphasized through comparative data, which validates teaching the actual skill to be learned. 2. Provide meaning to the performance through the suggestion of tips and hints that target specific aspects of the skill.
6	Eliciting the Performance	Practice	The skill is performed while the movements' boundaries are explored in order to produce the correct efficient movement pattern.	Eliminating the fear of failure and allowing the student fail. Through failure, the learner explores the movement pattern of the skill and strengthens their competency in the task. Tasks should be difficult.	practice, permanent, perform, explore, refine, produce, try, feel, move, shift, compare, like, effort, relax, confident	1. Create a safe learning environment, which accepts failure and promotes exploratory methods of learning the new skill. 2. Promote repetition through random practice vs. blocked practice.
7	Providing Feedback	Feedback	Other than online feedback made by the learners themselves, outside feedback from the instructor can influence proper skill execution.	Providing constructive information that is not overwhelming. Focus on cues that the individual learner can resonate with.	feel, understand, good, close, ownership, comfortable, progress, body, envision, relax	1. Establish trust and ask if the student wants help prior to offering feedback. 2. Allow the learner to ask questions. 3. Incorporate visual, haptic, and verbal feedback to target polymodal learning.
8	Assessing the Performance	Mechanism	Learned response has become habitual with confidence and a measureable degree of skill in the performance of the act.	Learners should be proficient enough to perform the task without receiving third person feedback via coaching or hints, however should still be supervised.	assembles, calibrates, constructs, dismantles, displays, manipulation, measures, organizes, sketches, refines	1. Allow the student to demonstrate what they have learned through performance. 2. The instructor should use objective analysis through the implementation of a set of measurable parameters/outcomes.
9	Promoting Automaticity	Complex Overt Response	The individual can perform a motor act that is considered complex because of the movement pattern required. A smooth, efficient, automatic, hesitation free performance is achieved consistently.	Allow the student to 'take ownership' as the skill becomes engrained. The performer can make online corrections that are needed for proper performance.	achieve, master, perform, expert, automatic, skilled, react, instilled, ingrained, precision, naturalization	1. Verbal cues, which resonate the greatest, are to be used by the instructor/coach to trigger the learned efficient movement pattern of the student. 2. Focus can be directed externally to enhance the automatic production of the movement pattern.
10	Enhancing Retention and Transfer	Adaptation	Movements can be modified to fit novel situations or can be combined into elaborate sequences with harmony and consistency.	Promotion of the transfer of the skill, or a combination of two or more skills to competitive/realistic settings and the application of the skill in new situations.	adapt, alter, customize, rearrange, vary, revise, reorganize, transfers, relative, retention, articulation	1. Incorporate retention and transfer tests into evaluation. 2. Arrange the practice environment to resemble the actual performance setting, constructing it as 'real' as possible & taking into account as many perceptual modalities as possible.
11	Exploratory Creativity	Origination	Combining previously learned movement patterns (general motor programs) to sequence & perform new complex forms of learned movements.	Allow the student to develop new forms of movement patterns by not confining the exploratory bounds of movement parameters.	arranges, rebuilds, designs, initiates, explore, originates, builds, combines, composes, revolutionize, constructs	1. Arrange for exposure to new tasks, or segmental versions of pre-exposed tasks, that require the student to link general motor programs together in order to produce successful performances. 2. Promote the creation of new routines or training programs.

Why should I learn about psychomotor learning?

It is important to consider that learning has an affective (emotional), cognitive and psychomotor component and to apply this concept to improve learning. This is important whatever a person is teaching.

We have had a lot of success at our university in applying movement to reading. Learners remember what they move to, whether it is multiplication rock, or acting out a sequence of birthdays as fractions. Moving helps learning.

Try moving and learning some new concept at the same time. Understanding the psychomotor context of learning helps also to understand experiential learning which also adds a physical basis to the learning.

References

Abedi, J., & O'Neil, H. F. (2005). Assessment of Noncognitive Influences on Learning. *Educational Assessment*, *10*(3), 147-151. doi:10.1207/s15326977ea1003_1

Belen'kii, V.Y., Gurfinkel, V.S., & Pal'tsev, Y.I. (1967). Elements of control of voluntary movements. *Biofizika, 12,* 135-141.

Blouin, J., Gauthier, G.M., Vercher, J.L., & Cole, J. (1996). The relative contribution of retinal and extraretinal signals in determining the accuracy of reaching movements in normal subjects and a deafferented patient. *Experimental Brain Research*, 109, 148-153.

Dave, R. (1967). Psychomotor domain. In *Berlin: International Conference of Educational Testing*.

Driscoll, M. P. (2005). Psychology of learning for instruction

Edgecombe, K., Seaton, P., Monahan, K., Meyer, S., LePage, S., & Erlam, G. (2013). Clinical simulation in nursing: A literature review and guidelines for practice.

Feil, P. (1992). An assessment of the application of psychomotor learning theory constructs in preclinical laboratory instruction. *Journal of dental education, 56*(3), 176-182.

Fitts, P.M., & Posner, M.I. (1967). *Human performance*. Belmont, CA: Brooks/Cole.

Gagne, RM., Briggs, LJ., Wager, WW. (1992). *Principles of instructional design.*

Harrow, A. (1972). A taxonomy of the psychomotor domain. *A guide for developing behavioral objectives*. New York: McKay.

Henry, F.M., & Rogers, D.E. (1960). Increased response latency for complicated movements and a "memory drum" theory of neuromotor reaction. *Research*

Quarterly, 31, 448-458."

Huitt, W. (2003). The psychomotor domain. *Educational Psychology Interactive.* Valdosta, GA: Valdosta State University. Retrieved April 14, 2015. http://www.edpsycinteractive.org/topics/behavior/psymtr . html.

Kawato, M., Furukawa, K., & Suzuki, R. (1987). A hierarchical neural-network model for control and learning of voluntary movement. *Biological Cybernetics, 57*(3), 169-185.

Khadjooi, K., Rostami, K., & Ishaq, S. (2011). How to use Gagne's model of instructional design in teaching psychomotor skills. *Gastroenterology and Hepatology From Bed to Bench, 4*(3), 116–119.

Laguador, J. M., & Ramos, L. R. (2014). Industry-partners' preferences for graduates: Input on curriculum development. *Journal of Education and Literature,* 1(1), 1-8.

McSparron, J. I., Michaud, G. C., Gordan, P. L., Channick, C. L., Wahidi, M. M., Yarmus, L. B., ... & Kovitz, K. L. (2015). Simulation for skills-based education in pulmonary and critical care medicine. *Annals of the American Thoracic Society, 12*(4), 579-586.

San Chee, Y., & Tan, K. C. D. (2012). Becoming chemists through game-based inquiry learning: The case of legends of alkhimia. *Electronic Journal of eLearning,* 10(2).

Schmidt, R. A. (1975). A schema theory of discrete motor skill learning. *Psychological Review, 82,* 225–260.

Schmidt, R.A., & Lee, T. D. (2014). *Motor Learning and Performance: From principles to application 5th edition.* Champaign, IL: Human Kinetics.

Simpson, E. J. (1966). The Classification of Educational Objectives, Psychomotor Domain. *Illinois Journal of Home Economics*. University of Illinois, Urbana.

Simpson, E. J. (1970). *The classification of educational objectives, psychomotor domain*. Department of Health, Education, and Welfare, Office of Edcn..

Slater-Hammel, A. T. (1960). Reliability, accuracy, and refractoriness of a transit reaction. *Research Quarterly. American Association for Health, Physical Education and Recreation, 31*(2), 217-228.

Taub, E. (1976). Movement in nonhuman primates deprived of somatosensory feedback. *Exercise and Sport Sciences Reviews, 4,* 335-374.

Taub, E., & Berman, A.J. (1968). Movement and learning in the absence of sensory feedback. In S.J. Freedman (Ed.), *The neuropsychology of spatially oriented behavior* (pp. 173-192). Homewood, IL: Dorsey.

Urbankova, A. (2010). Impact of computerized dental simulation training on preclinical operative dentistry examination scores. *Journal of Dental Education*, 74(4), 402-409.

Verdaasdonk, E. G. G., Stassen, L. P. S., Van Wijk, R. P. J., & Dankelman, J. (2007). The influence of different training schedules on the learning of psychomotor skills for endoscopic surgery. *Surgical Endoscopy*, 21(2), 214-219.

Vincent, M. A., Sheriff, S., & Mellott, S. (2015). The efficacy of high-fidelity simulation on psychomotor clinical performance improvement of undergraduate nursing students. *Computers Informatics Nursing*, 33(2), 78-84.

Wilson, L.O. (2003). The Psychomotor or Kinesthetic Domain. *The Second Principle.*

Chapter 5 - Experiential Learning

Julia Parra, Wanda Bulger-Tamez, Cynthia Gomez, & Mehmet Ozer

As noted, experiential learning (EL) has been around for centuries, since at least ancient Greece and China. In its modern incarnation, EL originated with John Dewey and his belief that children learn through experiencing their environment and natural inquiry. Montessori and Piaget contributed to that philosophy, arguing that children learn cognitively through social interaction and introduction to new ideas. Kolb further refined experiential learning as a six-stage process, combining recursive learning and creating knowledge through adaptations.

Dewey

John Dewey (1859-1952) believed in a naturalistic, environmental child-centered approach to learning. Teachers must identify experiences that will lead to meaningful experienced-based learning for each student. As learners experience their world they make connections for learning through scientific inquiry

John Dewey

While other theories focus on one aspect of learning such as a growth in intellectual knowledge experiential learning "emphasize[s] the central role that experience plays in the learning process, an emphasis that distinguishes it from other learning theories" (Sternberg, 2001, p. 227). Dewey embraced EL, proposing "that the native and unspoiled attitude of childhood, marked by ardent curiosity, fertile imagination, . . . [is] very near, to the attitude of the scientific mind" (Dewey, 1997, p. vii). This process of understanding new information stems from a scientific inquiry where experiences connected to learning shows learners how to rule out fallacies based on insufficient knowledge. Re-evaluation of experienced understandings may then be synthesized into a deep reflection.

Dewey studied at the University of Michigan under his mentor, George Sylvester Morris. Dewey founded a lab school at the University of Chicago and began to embrace pragmatism, which embodied a naturalistic approach between the interactions of individuals and their environment. There, Dewey described learning as "an active, transformative process in which concepts and experiences are seen as part of a larger, organic whole, and the role of logic as inquiry: . . . sorting, ordering, and categorizing qualities and traits of experiences with concepts as means that are themselves reconstituted in inquiry" (Johnston, 2014, p. 75).

John Dewey was not only instrumental in bringing the perspective of pragmatism into the naturalistic approach, he continued to gain popularity as a philosopher as well as an educational theorist and advocate for teachers. In "How We Think", Dewey laid the groundwork for teachers to build a systematic approach to teaching and a deep understanding of how a child learns. (Johnston, 2014, p. 125). This work led into his theory of knowledge, which is a method of thought and how we enact our own experience into the direction of new learning through reflection.

According to Dewey (1997), "experimental thinking or scientific reasoning is developed through an analysis and fusion of knowledge that is assimilated into previously learned ideas (Dewey, 1997" , p. 152), factual or not. Because thinking is a natural occurrence, teaching should keep students' minds active. Conversely, teaching can also stifle the learning process, which Dewey suggested happens when teachers maintain finite expected outcomes, rather than facilitate an extension or an alternative way beyond their own expectations. Dewey advocated an environment where students are encouraged to challenge assumptions and develop their own ways of making sense of content, predating - but predicting - constructivism.

In a prime example of similar but diverse thinking during the same period of time, Maria Montessori was advocating that teachers adopt an environment of child-centered learning similar to the one that John Dewey was arguing for

Maria Montessori

Maria Montessori

Italian theorist Maria Montessori (1870-1952) arguably has had more influence over early childhood education that any other theorist. While there may be relatively few "Montessori" schools, the influence of Maria Montessori can be seen in any early childhood classroom. Montessori, the first woman in Italy to graduate medical school, specialized in pediatrics. In her early career, she worked with children who were institutionalized for mental disabilities and were considered "untreatable". After observation and study, she concluded that the methods used by adults to treat these children were ineffective, so she asserted that these same children could learn under the right environmental conditions (Mooney, 2000).

In 1907, Dr. Montessori opened and directed a school in an especially poor district of Rome to provide a safe and nurturing place to keep children of working class parents off the streets. It was here that she began to develop her theories and methods of education. Although Montessori's ideas were revolutionary at the time, by 1913 a number of schools in the United States were using her methods.

Learning Theory

Montessori believed that children learn unconsciously from their environment insofar as they absorb and instruct themselves (Montessori, 1969). The teachers' role is to create a child-centered environment that promotes exploration, curiosity, and discovery. The child-centered environment should attend to both the physical space and activities designed. The furniture should be designed for ease of use by children, including tables, chairs, cupboards, shelf height, stairs, sinks, and so forth. It should be aesthetically pleasing and orderly for children to learn about beauty and order. The learning environment should also include real tools that are functional and can make things happen when children use them. Under her philosophy, children cannot learn to effectively use tools that are only designed to "pretend" play. All tools should be accessible to children so they can make decisions about when and how to use materials and tools. If the teacher brings out tools only when they are a part of a learning activity, the children will learn to depend on the teacher to choose the proper instruments for them. Montessori believed that tools should be accessible at all times to the students since they may need them for their own personal learning.

Montessori argued that children should be encouraged to care for themselves and their environment and believed that adults spent too much time serving them. She cautioned teachers to remember that children who are not allowed to do something for themselves do not learn how to do it (Mooney, 2000). Montessori saw many practical opportunities in the school day for children to learn, and to take care of themselves and the environment. These tasks included washing desks, organizing materials, learning to care for plants and animals, cooking, community service, and so forth – there were real jobs that were and still are meaningful to children. She believed that when children are involved in meaningful real-life work, rather than contrived tasks, they build a sense of self-efficacy and confidence. Also, when children are involved in practical and meaningful work, they are less likely to be disruptive.

The focus of Montessori's method is observation, which likely stems from her background as a doctor and scientist. Montessori teachers are trained to "teach little and observe much" (Mooney, 2000). Montessori believed that teachers need to understand and argued that understanding the interests and needs of children comes from careful observation. She believed that if children do not learn it is the result of adults not listening carefully or watching closely enough. Careful observation by the teacher is needed to plan the appropriate environment and curriculum that meets children's natural instructs to learn.

Implications for Curriculum and Methods of Teaching

Montessori's handbook suggests three important curricular

emphases – motor education, sensory education, and language development (Montessori, 1965). Motor education includes all things related to movement (walking, raising, sitting, handling objects), self-care, management of household, gardening, manual work, gymnastics, and rhythmic movement. Today those skills are still relevant for children to become self-sufficient, able to take responsibility for personal health, and become contributors within their community. Sensory education relates to activities that "educate the eye" and support students in trusting themselves to solve problems, develop critical thinking skills, and reflect on the effectiveness of their work. The types of activities designed for sensory education include stacking cylinders, using building blocks, ordering objects by size, and classifying shapes. The activities might look like play from an outside observer, but they are purposeful with the aim "that the child train himself to observe; that he will be able to make comparisons between objects, to form judgments, to reason and to [make decisions]" (Montessori, 2011, p. 33).

Language development is also purposefully planned in the curriculum. During play, which continues to be strongly advocated today as an important experiential learning tool (*see* Kohn, 2015), the teacher introduces words that describe the phenomena in which children are engaged and can add language descriptors that create order in the child's experience. For example, as children play with blocks, the teacher may purposefully use descriptors like *large* and *small*, or *thick* and *thin* to describe the blocks, repeatedly using the introduced language. Following the naming objects, the teacher should engage students in recognizing objects that fit the term, like, "Show me the small block?" Finally, the progression of language development moves to student pronunciation of words with prompts such as, "What is this?". Over time, the purposeful introduction of language provides a way for student to classify and categorize their world (Montessori, 1965).

Montessori's curricular approach, which provides an experiential structure for students to develop confidence in themselves as learners and contributors to society, and was quite different from that of another European, Jean Piaget. Piaget believed that children brought their language abilities to school with them and then learned from each other in the classroom environment.

Piaget

Jean Piaget (1896-1980) focused on the cognitive developmental process of the learner. He explains the process of learning using this perspective. According to Piaget, people have schemas in their minds based on their prior learning. Piaget believed that the human mind exists in a state of equilibrium and balance.

Jean Piaget

For example, when a child learns what a particular object is that is new, disequilibrium occurs until the child either assimilates or accommodates this new idea or image into his or her schema, after which equilibrium is restored. "Integration into a whole is an assimilation to a common structure, and the differentiations include assimilations which occur according to special conditions. The second central process is the accommodation that is the result of the necessity to consider the characteristics of the elements that are to be assimilated" (Piaget, 1978, pg. 6-7).

Stages of Learning

While interviewing children, Piaget became intrigued with how, at a certain age, students all seemed to get the same wrong answer. Piaget was more interested in how students were reasoning their answers than whether they were right or wrong (Kolb, 1984). The ways students at different ages arrived at similar and often incorrect answers caused Piaget to develop the well-known ideas of learning as first needing concrete objects, then representative forms, and finally understanding abstract and non-anchored thinking somewhere around the age of 12 or 13.

Piaget theorized how intelligence is shaped by experience. "Intelligence is not an innate internal characteristic of the individual but arises as a product of the interaction between the person and his or her environment" (Kolb, 2014, p. 12). With experiences students can individualize their learning and make it personal so the learning can become more permanent for them. Metacognition also occurs, wherein "the child [learns] about the process of discovering knowledge not, just the content" (Kolb, 2014, p. 14). When children are encouraged to pursue their own curiosity through rich experiences such "classrooms buzzed with the excitement and energy of intrinsically motivated learning activity" (Kolb, 2014, p. 14).

EL has changed the learning landscape. Kolb (1984) explains this situation as follows: These experience-based learning programs changed the educational process in two ways. First they altered the content of curriculum, providing new ways of teaching subjects that were formerly taught in inaccessible ways to young people and second they altered the learning process in ways that invite students to learn about new subjects.

Piaget believed that children think differently than adults and today most early childhood educators agree with him, although minorities contend that children think the same, but feel differently. However the majority of early educators agree with Piaget's cognitive development mental theories that children feel the same but think differently. Piaget identifies four stages applicable to all children in cognitive development. These stages are as follows (Piaget & Inhelder, 1969; Karkou, 2006):

Sensory Motor (0-2 ages): The child can only catch and suck at the beginning of this stage. As the time flows the child develops a sensory curiosity about the world. Child tries to identify and learn everything. Intelligence is demonstrated through motor activity without use of symbols.

- *Pre-operational* (2-7): The child starts to use symbolic thinking and develops language and uses it properly. Intelligence is demonstrated through use of symbols. He has a developed imaginary and memory but thinking is still non-logic. Thinking is egocentric.

- *Concrete operational* (7-11): Intelligence is demonstrated through logical and systematic manipulation of symbols related to concrete objects. Child can understand and apply abstract concepts like time, space and quantity but the need to be related to another concrete concept.

- *Formal operational* (11+): Intelligence is demonstrated thorough the logical use of symbols related to abstract concepts.

Piaget's stages of experiential learning would later be integrated into a more complex model proposed by educational theorist David Kolb, who included convergent and divergent thinking, as well as active experimentation and abstract conceptualization, within the cycle of learning.

David Kolb

Dr. David Kolb wrote about experiential learning during the early 1980's. His textbook *Experiential Learning: Experience as the Source Of Learning and Development* (1984) detailed the early work on experiential learning by other academics in the 1900's. Gardner's Multiple Intelligences provides a basis for understanding and using.

David Kolb

Kolb's learning concepts. Kolb is still Professor of Organizational Development at Case Western Reserve University, Cleveland, Ohio, where he continues to teach and researching in the fields of learning and development, adult development, experiential learning, learning style, and notably 'learning focused institutional development in higher education'

Kolb's Experiential Learning Theory (Learning Styles) Model

Kolb's learning theory describes four learning styles, which are based on a four-stage learning cycle. It explains the way individuals' different learning styles can be used as part of a cycle of experiential learning that applies to everyone. Kolb's "cycle of learning" is the central point of his experiential four-stage learning theory, in which 'immediate or concrete experiences' provide a basis for 'observations and reflections'. Observations and reflections, in turn, are assimilated and distilled into abstract concepts. Kolb's cycle (1984) is:

Concrete Experience (Apprehension) - (CE): Corresponds to "knowledge by acquaintance". There is direct practical experience for the learner. The learner is involved in exploration.

Reflective Observation - (RO): Corresponds to what the experience means to the experiencer (transformed by intension). The learner observes and, reflects on what is being observed.

- *Abstract Conceptualization* - (AC): Reflection gives rise to a new idea, or a modification of an existing abstract concept.
- *Active Experimentation* - (AE): The learner applies the learned experience to the real world.

His four-type definition of learning styles (1984) include:

- *Diverging* (CE/RO): Learner feels and watches. At this stage, the learner is usually in a nervous situation due to placement in a new situation and not knowing what he/she is going to do.
- *Assimilating* (AC/RO): Learner thinks and watches. The learner starts to understand and internalize the steps of the experience.
- *Converging* (AC/AE): Learner thinks and watches. At this stage the learner thinks on the experience and starts to do the actual experience.
- *Accommodating* (CE/AE): Feeling and doing. By this time, the learner's nervousness has been supplanted with confidence because the experience is accomplished and the learner was able to perform the experience.

Kolb discusses the increasing complexity and mechanization of the world and its effect on our lives. He offers education to be the solution of this problem: "we have cast our lot with learning and learning will pull us through. But this learning process must be re-imbued with the texture and feeling of human experiences shared and interpreted through dialogue with one another" (Kolb, 2014, p. 2). The method uses both andragogy and pedagogy, including computer classes, physical education classes, professional trainings, teacher preparation, in service education as well as many other platforms.

EL involves problem solving, critical thinking and active learning into the learning process. The learner is at the center of the learning process. It provides a permanence that is influenced by teachers, trainers, coaches, developers, administrators and many more people to influence their students or employees. The learning cycle is in the center of Kolb's learning style. The opportunities of reflection, observation and application of the learning helps to create a more permanent learning opportunity.

STEM and Identity-Based Experiential Learning Theory

A group of researchers at New Mexico State University in the Learning Technologies concentration within the Curriculum and Instruction department are working on developing projects (modules, grant development, etc.) using the Experiential Science Education Research Collaborative's (XSci) framework to support projects that are involved in the teaching, learning, and research of Science, Technology, Engineering and Mathematic (STEM) concepts (XSci, n.d.). The home of XSci is the University of Colorado Boulder's Center for STEM Learning. Make sure to visit the XSci website for further information about their framework and many projects (see http://www.xsci.org/).

The team developing these projects at NMSU is led by Dr. Julia Parra who experienced this transformative framework at the *Xperience STEM Conference* presented by XSci during Summer 2014 in Denver, Colorado. Currently, the XSci framework includes-1) Identity-Based Experiential Learning Theory (ID-Belt), 2) Experiential Learning Theory, 3) Narrative Study of Lives, and 4) Science Identity Construction (XSci, n.d.).

According to Kolb (2014), "human beings are unique among all living organisms in that their primary adaptive specialization lies not in some particular physical form or skill or fit in an ecological niche, but rather identification with the process of adaptation itself- in the learning" (p. 1). Experiential learning theory as noted by XSci (n.d.)

71

builds on Kolb's and other researcher perspectives and is further discussed "as a philosophy of education, in contrast to learning methodologies such as didactic or rote learning that are mostly concerned with knowledge delivery" and "concerned with learning from direct first-person experience and a holistic perspective that goes beyond content to include the construction of knowledge, attitudes, beliefs, and transfer of learning"(Marlow & McLain, 2011, p. 2). XSci's Operational Definition of Experiential Learning is, "[a] transactional learning strategy in which participants engage in direct experience and focused reflection, in concert with private personal interpretative processes on the part of the learner, to construct knowledge, develop skills, and contextualize the meaning of the experience" (XSci, n.d.).

As noted, experiential learning theory stands on over a hundred years of research and another two or three thousand years of educational philosophy. It is likely the oldest form of learning there is and yet grossly underutilized in education today. Experiential education is best understood as a philosophy of education, in contrast to learning methodologies such as didactic standards-based rote learning that is mostly concerned with content delivery.

Identity-based experiential learning, in particular, is concerned with learning from direct first-person experience and a holistic perspective that goes beyond content to include the construction of knowledge, attitudes and beliefs, the transfer of learning to new situations, personal relevance, meaning making, and identity development.

As such, experiential education offers an alternative approach to learning for both in-school and out-of-school environments. It comes in many disguises today, including play- based learning, problem-based learning, discovery learning, hands-on learning, service learning, inquiry-based learning, project-based learning, expeditionary learning, unschooling, and more. Several experientially based schools and programs have been pioneering in this direction for years - but mostly as private or specially sponsored endeavors free from the constraints of funding-related adherence to standards. Examples include: Expeditionary Learning Schools nationwide, The Journey School in Santa Fe, the Sudbury Valley School in Massachusetts, The Watershed School in Colorado, the Lake Travis STEM Academy in Texas, Jane Goodall's Roots & Shoots program in over 100 countries, LEGO Robotics, and many others.

Any practical pedagogy of identity-based experiential learning must include signature elements that are learner-centered as its highest priority. Such experiential characteristics, by definition, are holistic and intertwined in nature - encompassing the rich and multi-dimensional nature of human experience, rather than the somewhat arbitrary traditional segmentation of education into specific disciplines and associated standards

A key component of XSci's framework, as related to experiential learning, is the Experiential Learning Variables and Indicators Scale (ELVIS), which is, " a tool for designing and assessing teaching and learning efforts in terms of their "experiential-ness" and "synthesizes many of the best-known and well-researched models for experiential learning and boils them down into a very practical instrument that includes seven core characteristics of experiential learning: These characteristics include 1) locus of control, 2) physical involvement, 3) intellectual involvement, 4) social & emotional involvement, 5) narrative transport, 6) perceived risk, and 7) embedded reflection" XSci (n.d.).

ELVIS (EXPERIENTIAL LEARNING VARIABLES AND INDICATORS SCALE)

7 CHARACTERISTICS OF EXPERIENTIAL LEARNING	EXPERIENTIAL SCORE (1 = LOW, 5 = HIGH)				
	1	2	3	4	5
PERCEIVED RISK	NO OPPORTUNITY TO TAKE PHYSICAL, EMOTIONAL OR INTELLECTUAL RISK		MODERATE PHYSICAL, EMOTIONAL, OR INTELLECTUAL RISK		HIGH PHYSICAL, EMOTIONAL, OR INTELLECTUAL RISK
LOCUS OF CONTROL	EDUCATOR DIRECTED		EQUALLY EDUCATOR DIRECTED AND LEARNER DIRECTED		LEARNER DIRECTED
SENSORY & KINESTHETIC ACTIVATION	SEDENTARY		EQUALLY ACTIVE (HANDS ON) & SEDENTARY		COMPLETELY ACTIVE (HANDS-ON)
SOCIAL & EMOTIONAL INVOLVEMENT	1/5 ISOLATED	2/4	3 EQUALLY COLLABORATIVE & ISOLATED	4/2	5/1 COLLABORATIVE
INTELLECTUAL INVOLVEMENT	REACTIVE (BEING TALKED TO)		BOTH EQUALLY REACTIVE AND PRO-ACTIVE		PRO-ACTIVE (PROBLEM-BASED LEARNING)
NARRATIVE TRANSPORT	CLASSROOM BASED PERSPECTIVE		BOTH EQUALLY CLASSROOM BASED PERSPECTIVE AND IMMERSION		FULL IMMERSION
EMBEDDED REFLECTION	NO REFLECTION OR OR ACCIDENTAL REFLECTION PERIODS		MODERATE STRUCTURED & EMBEDDED REFLECTION		HIGHLY STRUCTURED AND EMBBEDED REFLECTION PERIODS

Importantly, rather than functioning like traditional instructional rubrics (such as standards-based checklists, learning progressions, or pacing guides), the seven variables of the ELVIS instrument describe environmental and experiential elements (such as "are there opportunities for learners to take physical, emotional, or intellectual risks?") that are not "instructed" or "taught" so much as facilitated and/or designed into the learning experience. This indicates an entirely different role for educators than traditionally held--that of crafting (much like an artist) the right conditions, opportunities, and experiences for discovery and self-discovery, ultimately based on an understanding of individual students' identities. Again, the emphasis remains on the learner's individual experience, which may indeed include specific content or skills as described in standards, but only as one element among many, comprising a meaningful learning experience.

Identity-based experiential learning design casts educators in the role of guide rather than lecturer. Experiential educators need to facilitate the transformation of knowledge into understanding through familiarity with experiential learning theory, identity development, and the narrative construction of meaning and personal relevance to what is learned. This is a new perspective and skill set for most educators.

A central focus of this work is, of course, identity construction. Applied to education, it is the idea that the learning of new things can go beyond their incorporation into internal frameworks (or schema) for understanding, as traditional theories suggest, to actually inform, modify, and become integrated into a person's identity or identities. Simply put... learning changes us, sometimes deeply. Identity theory incorporates the self into the learning equation and considers the relationship of the "knower" to the "known" as an essential element to all learning, personal meaning making, agency, inspiration, and ultimately action. In particular, XSci has studied science identity construction – or the psychological processes by which people become inspired by science, engineering, technology, and mathematics (STEM) through experiences to the point of personal relevance, ownership, and integration into the sense of self.

Accordingly, science identity construction is the forging of a personally relevant relationship to science in the form of an identity out of which meaning is made and modified over time. Where standards define science literacy as success, this view positions a positive science identity as a critical precursor (and outcome) of qualitative approaches to education. For our teachers, identity-based professional development can enrich their self-concepts and capacities as passionate professionals able to ignite lifelong curiosity and inspiration within their students.

The lens of identity-based experiential learning and its emphasis on learner-centered perspectives has also taken XSci beyond STEM education and into the broader implications for learning in general. To date, this work has resulted in a new conceptual framework that situates narrative as the mediator between experience and identity as the predominant pathway for meaning making and the establishment of personal relevance to learning, a relatively innovative concept within educational contexts.

The XSci team's work with their projects has led to the development of a research-based tool, the Science Identity Scale, that when completed, "will serve as a quantitative instrument for use with larger samples for characterizing an individual's integration of science into his/her sense of self" (Merck Foundation [MF], 2014, p. 39). The Science Identity Scale has its foundation in a framework, the science identity construction zone, that places the focus on learners -- at the center. These may be students or educators in professional development situations. According to MF (2014), the zones in this model articulate "different areas of personal growth and learning (cognitive and non-cognitive) as science identity construction." Further, these zones include: "Agency (or belief in one's capabilities); Content confidence (with the STEM content in the project): Emotional connection, and: Personal relevance."

In order to provide an example of curriculum based on the STEM and Identity-Based Experiential Learning, Dr. Parra developed the following professional development curriculum draft for an upcoming grant project:

Julia Parra

DAY 1: SETTING UP

Adventurers (teachers) will:

- Receive Adventure Backpacks including-hat, water, sunscreen, snacks, pens, Field Guide (Notebook with Handouts for concepts including ELVIS, pedagogical models, storyboards for narrative documentary, QR codes for further online resources, and so on.), copy of XSci documentary video, Inspire Me! AFRICA, iPad, GoPro Hero Camera and accessories, Lego pack for introduction and question/answer activities.

- Engage with the related Pedagogical Models using handouts and digital models to start developing curriculum ideas for their own teaching and learning environments.

- Explore documentary story-telling strategies and techniques (including the phases of pre-production, production, and post-production as well as narrative construction) in preparation for developing documentaries.

DAY 2: LAKE ADVENTURE & DOCUMENTARY DEVELOPMENT

This lake adventure combines the exciting sport of Stand-Up-Paddleboarding and/or Kayaking (no experience necessary) with STEM activities and documentary filmmaking using Go-Pro camera systems. This experience includes an educational cross section of geography, lake and marine ecology, the physics of buoyancy and hydrodynamic design, documentary filmmaking and STEM-related personal narrative development, Go-Pro camera operation, and editing software.

Adventurers will:

- Engage in concept mapping and question asking (and prepare for data collection and manipulation?)

- Explore the geography of Elephant Butte Lake with maps, satellite imaging, and robots

- Stand-up-paddleboard or kayak on Elephant Butte Lake
- Learn proper safety, equipment, and techniques (balance, turning, strokes, falling, and recovery and including conversations regarding the physics of buoyancy and hydrodynamic design, issues of water, and so on.)
- Explore and respect the lake and marine environment with this low-impact sport (including water sampling and analysis for algal blooms, pH, phosphorous and other trace nutrients)
- Use a Go-Pro camera system to record experiences
- Use ELVIS to evaluate the experiential nature of this activity

DAYS 3 & 4: POST EXTRAORDINARY EXPERIENCE ACTIVITIES
Adventurers will:
- Create Documentary Video (Engage in post-production and narrative construction to edit and share personal documentary shorts in high definition)
- Engage in post-experience activities to support reflection and the take-aways for personal individualized classroom use.
- Collaboration partners, XSci and National Geographic Society have many existing STEM curricula to draw from to create a menu of STEM extraordinary experiences for teacher professional development intervention.

In summary, EL has been proven to be one of the most powerful ways to learn as it vastly improves long-term retention over exposure via lecture or lecture and discussion. Play and role-play cannot be overstated in improving learners' thinking skills and willingness to experiment with the risk of making mistakes and learning outside their comfort zones. Exercises and simulations that have a purpose give learners an emotional investment in learning content and process, particularly when they involve a real-life scenario followed by a debriefing, reflection and self-assessment.

Experiential based learning overlaps to a significant degree with social constructivism, as both stress the importance of an interactive educational environment which is simultaneously intellectually, linguistically and socially stimulating as well as student-centered.

Why should I learn about experiential learning?

Think back to when you were a student in school. What do you remember as significant learning experiences?

Almost always these were experiences in which you went on a field trip or when you created a play or built an adobe church or settlement?

Experiences engage us much more than just reading about something in a text book. Contrast the #1 with #2 and #3:

1. Please turn to page 312 and read about the early pioneers in our state.
2. Imagine you are part of an early wagon train traveling across the desert. You are running low on water, your mother is very sick, your father has gone ahead to scout out a place to camp. How do you feel? What will you do?
3. You are part of an indigenous group of people who have always lived peacefully next to a raging river in Northern New Mexico. You have built a village of homes out of the sides of cliffs. Your father is off hunting and your mother is ill and suddenly a group of strange looking men in dark blue uniforms are approaching your village. How do you feel? What do you do?

References

Dewey, J. (1997). *How we think.* Boston: DC. Dover Publications, Inc.Johnston, J. S. (2014). *John Dewey's earlier logical theory.* Albany: NY. State University of New York Press

Karkou, V. (2006). *Arts therapies: A research-based map of the field.* Elsevier Health Sciences

Kohn, D. 16 May 2015. Let the Kids Learn Through Play. *The New York Times*, accessed 18 May 2015 at http://www.nytimes.com/2015/05/17/opinion/sunday/let-the-kids-learn-through-play.html

Kolb, D. (1984). *Experiential learning: Experience as the source of learning and development.* Englewood Cliffs, N.J.: Prentice-Hall.

Kolb, D. (2014). *Experiential learning: Experience as the source of learning and development.* Upper Saddle River, N.J: Pearson Education, Inc.

Marlow, M. P., & McLain, B. (2011). Assessing the impacts of experiential learning on teacher classroom practice. *Research in Higher Education Journal, 14*, 1- 15.

Merck Foundation. (2014). Extraordinary educator experiences. Retrieved from http://www.xsci.org/wp-content/uploads/2015/01/FINAL-Merck-Year-3-Report.pdf

Montessori, M. (1965). *Dr. Montessori's own handbook.* New York: Schocken Books.

Montessori, M. (1969). *The absorbent mind Translated from the Italian by Claude A. Claremont.* ([7th ed.). Thiruvanmiyur: Kalakshetra.

Montessori, M. (2011). *Dr. Montessori's own handbook.* Schocken

Mooney, C. (2000). *Theories of childhood: An introduction to Dewey, Montessori, Erikson, Piaget and Vygotsky.* St. Paul, MN: Redleaf Press.

Piaget, J. (1977). Problems of Equilibrium. In Appel, M., & Goldberg, L. (editors) *Topics in cognitive development.* (3-15) New York:

Plenum Press.

Piaget, J. (1977). *The development of thought: Equilibration of cognitive structures.* New York: Viking Press.

Piaget, J. (1978). *Behavior and evolution* (D. Nicholson-Smith, Trans.) New York: Random House. (Original work published 1976).

Piaget, J., & Inhelder, B. (1969). *The psychology of the child.* Basic Books.

Sternberg, R. J. (2001). *Perspectives on thinking, learning, and cognitive styles.* New York: NY. Routledge

Additional Readings

Annetta, L. A., Murray, M., Laird, S., Bohr, S., & Park, J. (2006). Serious games: Incorporating video games in the classroom. *Educause Quarterly*, 16-22.

Bandura, A. (1997). *Self-efficacy: The exercise of control.* New York, NY: W.H. Freeman and Company.

Bransford, B., & Brown, A. L. Cocking (1999). *How people learn: Brain, mind, experience, and school.* Washington, DC: National Research Council.

Breuer, J. S., & Bente, G. (2010). Why so serious? On the relation of serious games and learning. Eludamos. *Journal for Computer Game Culture*, 4(1), 7-24.

Brown, J. S., Collins, A., & Duguid, P. (1989). Situated cognition and the culture of learning. *Educational Researcher*, 18(1), 32-42.

Caine, R. N., & Caine, G. (1990). Understanding a brain-based approach to learning and teaching. *Educational Leadership*, 48(2), 66-70.

Caine, R. N., & Caine, G. (1991). *Making connections: Teaching and the human brain*. Alexandria, VA: Association for Supervision and Curriculum Development.

Caine, R. N., & Caine, G. (1995). Reinventing schools through brain-based learning. *Educational Leadership*, 52, 43-43.

Caine, R. N., & Caine, G. (1997). *Unleashing the power of perceptual change: The potential of brain-based teaching*. Alexandria, VA: Association for Supervision and Curriculum Development.

Chambers, D. (1993) Images are both depictive and descriptive. In B. Roskos-Ewoldson, M. Intons-Peterson, & R. Anderson (Eds.), *Imagery, creativity, and discovery: A cognitive perspective* (pp.77-97). Netherlands: Elsevier.

Chamberlin, B., Trespalacios, J. & Gallagher, R. (2012) The learning games design model: Immersion, collaboration, and outcomes-driven development. *International Journal of Game-Based Learning*.

Chamberlin, B., Trespalacios, J., & Gallagher, R. (2014). *Bridging research and game development: A learning games design model for multi-game projects virtual learning environments and game-based education: methodologies, tools, and curriculum design*. Hershey, PA: IGI Global, forthcoming.

Clements, D. & Sarama, J. (2009) *Learning and teaching early math; The learning trajectories approach*. New York: NY: Erlbaum.

Clement, J., Lochhead, J., and Monk, G. (1981). Translation difficulties in learning mathematics. *American Mathematical Monthly*, 88(4), 286-290.

Chapter 6 - Social Constructivist Learning Theory

Pamela Duncan & Cynthia Gomez

Social constructivist theory extends constructivism (see Chapter 4) to include students' social interactions within the classroom and with culture at large (Van de Walle, Karp, & Bay-Williams, 2010). Educational theory pioneers Lev Vygotsky and Paolo Freire embodied the understanding of the psychology of learning and the humanizing of education wherein teachers "ask themselves for whom and on whose behalf they are working" (Freire, 1985, p. 80).

Lev Vygotsky

Lev Vygotsky (1896-1934), studied medicine and then law at Moscow University and his contributions to education were interdisciplinary (Cooper, 2002). Vygotsky researched human psychological development and - in an idea controversial for its time - opposed *rote* learning because it did not engage children in an interactive meaning-making process and failed

Lev Vygotsky

to connect them with the social aspects of the world around them (Scott, 2008). Vygotsky stressed the importance of play between an adult and a child, or more importantly among children, because it helps develop their understanding of social rules and expectations. Such socialization encourages the development of higher cognitive abilities, which promotes learning in the future. For example, language is learned in social settings and through mentoring relationships.

Although Vygotsky died at age 37 of tuberculosis, his contributions retain much significance today.

The Zone of Proximal Development

One underpinning of social constructivist theory is the Zone of Proximal Development (ZPD). Vygotsky defined ZPD as, "The distance between the actual developmental level as determined by independent problem solving and the level of potential development as determined through problem solving under adult guidance or in collaboration with more capable peers" (Vygotsky, 1978, p. 86). The level of actual development is what students can do independently, while the level of potential development is what the student is capable of doing with scaffolding and collaboration with adults or peers. ZPD creates the opportunity for peer tutoring and collaboration within a classroom and demonstrates that a student has the ability to learn content through collaboration. The ZPD concept also demonstrates a view of intelligence as a fluid process of knowledge creation and retention that is difficult to assess using traditional methods.

Vygotsky's child-centrism was groundbreaking even by the revolutionary standards established by the new Russian political regime. But while Vytogsky's theories were neither inherently, nor intentionally political, those of Paulo Freire would very much be, explicitly so.

Paulo Freire

Paulo Freire (1921-1997) battled illiteracy and many other social injustices in his native Brazil. He introduced critical pedagogy to educational learning, principles which are embedded in the combination of language, thought, and culture. In addition, his "anti-colonialist stance not only [sought] to transcend individualistic.

Paulo Freire

transformations, commonly encouraged by liberal education, but more importantly, . . encourage[d] a practical collective engagement to bring about social change" (Martinez-Salazar, 1998, p.129). His theory presupposes that people may be controlled and suppressed by denying them access to education. Put another way, education was a political undertaking that involves the use of the educational system to control people through social systems of oppression (Schugurensky, 1998).

By 1964, Freire was living in exile, eventually residing in the United States before returning 15 years later to a more democratic Brazil. He argued that instruction must be provided in such a way that allows the learner to take charge of his or her learning. Some of the many contributions that Freire made to education include the idea of "banking education" under which a teacher provides students with instruction that is supplanted to the extent that the teacher deems fit, without encouraging students to reflect or think for themselves. Under "problem-posing education", students actively engage in thinking and synthesize prior knowledge (Freire, 2005, p. 22). In *Pedagogy of the Oppressed* Freire argues that when students develop deeper understanding, they build a "critical consciousness of the social, political and economic contradictions and may take action against them" (Freire, 1970, p. 43).

Application

Social Constructivist Theory has applications in many educational settings. Vygotskian theory suggests that when teachers introduce a new topic they should scaffold the learning according to each students' ZPD. It follows that teachers should ascertain what the students currently know in order to *scaffold* the learning by breaking down large topics into smaller segments to make concepts and ideas more manageable and to provide different entry points for the learning for the students.

Technology can be used as a way to carry some of the cognitive load of a complex topic while students are learning. For example, a student can navigate the learning of new and complex content via computer and guided inquiry. Scaffolding aligns with the model of apprenticeship learning, wherein experts slowly guide students through the learning process of a topic by increasingly delegating responsibilities until they no longer need apprenticeship. Because of the importance of discourse, teachers need to use and apply a wide vocabulary so that students can assimilate it into their mental schema for any given topic. Teachers should also encourage students to ask questions and participate in discussion so students become familiar and comfortable with academic language. Collaborative activities are essential for students' social and cognitive development. They should be given tasks that encourage exploration and discovery of a topic, while a teacher should provide guiding questions rather than emphasizing or providing "correct" answers.

Why should I learn about Social Constructivist Learning Theory?

Over the last 20 years psychologists, educators, and learning scientists have learned a great deal about how people learn. New views of learning include an understanding of how social interactions, as well as cultural and political contexts influence what is learned and how it is learned. It is important to understand these new perspectives on learning for those who are teaching, managing learning environments, and creating new instructional materials.

We need to understand better how social and cultural contexts influence learning for all students. The most important question to ask is:

Are all of our students getting access to the best possible learning environments?

What strategies can we use to provide culturally and personally positive learning experiences for all?

References

Cooper, D. (2002-09-11). *Fifty modern thinkers on education: From Piaget to the present day.* London: Taylor and Francis. Kindle Edition

Freire, P. (1970). *Pedagogy of the oppressed.* London; The Continuum International Publishing Group, Inc.

Freire, P. (1985). *The politics of education: culture, power, and liberation.* (D. Macedo Translates). South Hadley, MA: Bergin & Gavey.

Freire, P. (2005). *Teachers as cultural workers; Letters to those who dare teach.* Boulder, CO: Westview Press.

Martinez-Salazar, E. (1998). Freire in the north under southern eyes. *Journal of Convergence Tribute to Paulo Freire,* XXX1 (1 & 2), 127-136.

Schugurensky, D. (1998). The legacy of Paulo freire: a critical review of his contributions. *Journal of Convergence Tribute to Paulo Freire,* XXX1 (1 & 2), 17-19.

Scott, D. (2008). *Critical essays on major curriculum theorists.* London: Taylor and Francis. Kindle Edition

Van de Walle, J.A, Karp, K.S, & Bay-Williams, J.M. (2010). *Elementary and middle school mathematics: Teaching*

Vygotsky, L. (1978). *Mind in society.* London: Harvard University Press.

Chapter 7 - Brain-based Learning

J.T. Knight, Gaspard Mucundanyi & Karin Wiburg

With the advancement in the study of learning using imaging technology, we can now actually see how the brain is working. Brain imagery allows scientists to see which parts of the brain are responding during learning. When children are born they have relatively evenly distributed neurons with little connections. As learners interact with the world, they grow clusters of neurons based on how the child interacts with his or her environment. It is interesting that early ideas about learning such as schemas (connected ideas on a topic) have proven true in the laboratory; particular parts of the brain respond to specific ideas and objects. Increased blood flow between the right and left hemispheres occurs among creative people; when students are answering simple questions only a small area of the brain lights up, and when they are thinking about a really complex problem, many more parts of the brain light up.

Brain-based learning is a concept based on what cognitive science has found out about how a person learns. By understanding how the brain changes physically when a person learns, a teacher can facilitate certain kinds of activities to support cognitive processing. There is persuasive evidence that the brain best remembers experiences that include representations, emotional meaning and connections to current learning. This concept of a continually learning brain calls in the question of the traditional view of intelligence as a fixed quantity, which does not change much during the human lifespan. "The learning of specific tasks appears to alter the specific regions of the brain involved in the task . . . the brain is a dynamic organ, shaped to a great extent by experience—by what a living being does, and has done" (Bransford, Brown, Cocking, & National Research Council (U.S.),1999, p. 126)

While there has been an explosion of writing about how the brain works in recent years and some work has been accomplished related to understanding learning as a result of brain functioning, there have only been a few attempts to help teachers to use brain-based theory in teaching. This chapter introduces some ideas about brain-based learning, neuropsychology, and the learning cycle, including short-term and long-term memory. Then, in the spirit of Robert Gagne who first connected the internal events of the learner with instructional events, connections between brain functioning and ways to facilitate brain functions during learning are discussed.

Neuropsychology

Neuropsychology is the study of the "relationships between the brain and behavior" (Heilman & Satz, 1983, p. 1). Educators who study neuropsychology hope to understand what motivates the different behaviors of students in their classes and how to improve their learning activities. Looking directly at brain functioning is often used for studying students with disabilities but it is also useful for studying the learning of all students because learning is influenced by behavior activated by the brain.

Different neuronal networks that are in charge of activating behavior compose the brain. There was a tremendous growth in the study of human thinking as the potential of studying brain functioning as somewhat similar to computer processing grew as a field in the 1980's. Thompson, Berger, & Berry (1980) explain that neurons play a role that is very similar to how a computer operates.

> *A neuron receives information from many sources (sensation) in ways that are very similar to the function of input on a computer; the neuron integrates this information (processing); neurons may be altered or 'store' the information (memory), and neurons transmit this information to other neurons, muscles, or internal organs (action or behavior)* (p. 4)

and finally actions or behavior are the output. Generally speaking, the brain's left hemisphere is responsible for language and speech while the right side deals with visual-spatial information (Heilman & Satz, 1983; Thompson, Berger, & Berry, 1980).

There are many different levels to the brain that are activated in different situations. The primal level, or "reptilian" brain, is triggered by fear-based, fight-or-flight scenarios, and overrides other brain processes. The middle, or "mammalian" brain, is where emotions reside. At the highest level is the neocortex, where the brain processes language and visual images and ideas. Ideally, the brain functions are integrated as learning occurs; ideas pass between the brain's hemispheres and within its lobes where they are formed into coherent and meaningful thoughts and sentences. When the brain is integrated from top to bottom learners feel safe and are able to better engage in learning. This is why, through multiple neural channels, learners remember ideas that were discovered or emotions encountered after hard work or the accomplishment of a specific project.

Hence, neuropsychology as applied to learning can help teachers to understand different behaviors of students in classes and how to improve their processes for learning activities. While neuropsychology historically has mainly been reserved for students with learning disabilities, it is applicable to and benefits all learners.

History of neuropsychology

People began to study neuropsychology as early as the 16th century although they had very primitive ways of doing this such as feeling bumps on the head. Rene Descartes (1596-1650) proposed a long-lasting theory that many people have suggested *separated the mind from the body*, proposing that "it is the soul that sees…and not the eye; and only by means of the brain does the immediate of seeing take place" (Kenny,1968, p. 218). By way of example, he referenced a girl whose arm continued to feel pain in a finger on an amputated arm. In Cartesian dualism the brain and mind are separate entities, but united because each cannot exist independent of the other. Descartes (incorrectly) believed that the pineal gland was "suspended" in the center of the brain and that it was the source of "animal spirits". His observation of a pattern of nerve fibers emanating from the gland put him well ahead of his time.

In the 19th century, Franz-Josef Gall (1758-1828) declined an offer of becoming the physician to emperor Franz II in order to continue his research into "why students who excelled in languages or had good memories also seemed (to him, at least) to have 'large prominent eyes'" (De, 1975, p. 13). He concluded that "the mind could be studied anatomically" (De, 1975, p. 13) and went on to propose the pseudoscience of phrenology, which was based on the idea that the brain is composed by different organs with psychological traits, which correspond to locations on the skull.

Jean-Baptiste Bouillaud (1796-1881), a distinguished French physician, found a direct correlation between speech disturbance and frontal (anterior) lobe damage that left other mental and physical faculties unaffected. Paul Broca (1884-1880), a surgeon, discovered that the language and speech are processed by the brain's left hemisphere by performing autopsies on speech- and language- impaired individuals, revealing damage to the brain's lower left frontal lobe. That locus became known as "Broca's area" (Konnikova, 2013).

Neurobiology and understanding student behavior

FMRI (functional magnetic resonance imaging) is a technology that allows researchers to view patterns in brain activity in real time, including interactions between two individuals such as a mother and her infant. In this way, we can see over long periods of time how and where neuron pathways are built by various stimuli and when the progression of such pathways slows down or stops.

Such brain scans, coupled with historical anecdotes of traumatic brain injuries that predate modern technology, have confirmed with precision where certain decision making faculties of the brain are. Depending on the severity of the injury and the age at which it occurs, the brain can compensate for loss in one area to redirect learning to other areas.

Application of neuropsychology to children with special needs

Fagan, Pisoni, Horn, and Dillon (2007) found that among children who were born deaf and subsequently received a cochlear implant between the ages of one and six, cognitive processes improved with respect to "NEPSY" neuropsychological assessments. In a study of elementary school children with serious behavioral and emotional problems, Mattison, Hooper, & Carlson (2006) argued that the NEPSY test would assist teachers of such students with intervention planning.

Assistive technology enables blind students to use computers to complete their assignments. This is an example of differential instruction which "can modify the brain, enabling it to use alternative sensory input to accomplish adaptive functions" (Bransford et al., 1999, p. 123). Some such students may even find they prefer do their assignments and exams on computers instead of writing in Braille on papers.

Application of neuropsychology in education generally

Neuropsychology demonstrates that "guided learning and learning from individual experiences both play important roles in the functional reorganization of the brain" (Bransford et al., 1999, p. 123). This approach to psychology can provide insight into the learning behavior of students, and explain when and why teaching strategies must be adjusted to provide an more appropriate learning environment for each student.

The brain develops in different phases and according to the different ages of a child. For example, at the age of three years, about 80 percent of brain growth is complete (D'arcangelo, 2000), but much of the brain remains differentiated into clusters of neurons and many ideas are not well developed. Changes in the brain continue to occur during the life span of a person. In a classroom, some students may present slow learning behaviors in their learning activities such as inability to speak which could be related to poor development or other factors. For example: The children between 3 and 12 years of age are able to learn 50 words per day and after 12 years of age the child faces challenges to learn words; that is why it is easy for young children to learn a new language comparatively to old people. On one hand, students may face learning problems based on lack of training during critical periods for learning language and mathematics; on the other hand, a student may have suffered a traumatic brain injury. Hence, the teacher needs to understand and deal with causes that can impede learning without appropriate intervention.

As previously noted, The Zone of Proximal Development (ZPD) is the difference between what a child can do without guidance or help with what she can learn with guidance (Vygotsky, 1986). Understanding memory functions and the brain may guide teachers as to what the students can do alone and determine activities which need to be done with the guidance by teachers and parents. With this knowledge, teachers can put students within their Zone of Proximal Development (ZPD) (Vygotsky, 1986; Darling-Hammond & Bransford, 2005).

Finally, the brain has short-term and long-term memories which operate like the computer's memories, Random Access Memory (RAM) is considered as short memory and a hard disk as long-term memory in a computer.

Short summary: Memory hierarchy in brain vs. computer memory

Computer	Human	
	Sensory memory	*It stores automatically the information that it perceives without paying attention for example in one second.*
Random Access Memory	Short-term memory	*Once a person pays attention to the information, it is stored in this memory for few minutes or lesser than minutes*
Hard disk	Long –term memory	*Once the information is kept for a long time in a short memory, it is transferred to long-term memory for days, months, and years*

Connecting Brain-based Learning and Teaching Strategies

There has been an explosion of writing about brain-based learning in recent years and some work has been accomplished related to understanding learning as a result of brain functioning. However, there have only been a few attempts to help teachers to use brain-based theory in teaching. This short section provides a symbolic picture of the functions of different parts of the brain during learning.

Below is a classical picture of the brain and learning functions, which reflects a cognitive and brain-based view of learning. Each of the numbers corresponds to what happens during learning for the learner. The learner must first perceive the learning intentions from cues from the teacher or presented material. So the first task for the brain is to focus attention on the learning task at hand. This may be the reason that administrators suggest to teachers to list the learning objective or goal for a lesson, although just listing the objectives may not be of interest to the learner and may not get the necessary attention. The outcomes are mostly for the teacher as the beginning. It is usually better to do some kind of Launch to the lesson that is of interest to a student, a puzzling action to be figured out, an interesting image, a short video. Later the teacher can then suggest to the student or ask the students to think about how the Launch was connected to the Learning goal.

Then the learner must play with the new ideas or concepts while in the working memory. Using multiple modalities, movement, music, images, and print, as well as emotions, helps the learner to encode concepts and ideas in short term memory, which will facilitate possible interactions with the schemas that

98

exist in long-term memory.

The key to supporting student learning is to support students in encoding concepts in long-term learning in ways that are later retrievable. As a teacher you can provide cues and suggestions, but the learner should be doing the work of learning and thinking, since active engagement in learning is the most important key to later retrieving what was learned during a lesson. Below is a classical picture of brain functioning. Each of the numbers correspond to what happens during learning from paying attention to encoding in short term memory to encoding in long-term memory and facilitating actions between the short term working memory and the long-term storage memory. While a teacher can provide cues and suggestions, the learner's active role of thinking is the most important key to later retrieving what was learned.

Connecting Brain-based Learning to Teaching

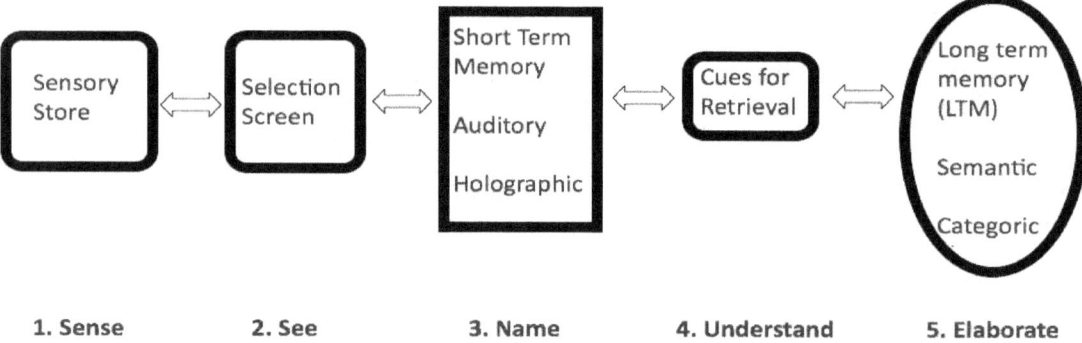

1. Sense　　**2. See**　　**3. Name**　　**4. Understand**　　**5. Elaborate**

Manipulate, Evaluate, Compare, Contrast, Analyze

This model of learning was developed by Karin M. Wiburg during her years of teaching educators about brain-based learning. Copyright, 1990, K.Wiburg.

　　1. **Gaining attention** is a lot harder than it sounds. Some students may have trouble paying attention or may have trouble with visual or auditory processing. There are very simple ways to test this in a few minutes with an entire class. Using a simple overhead projector the teacher can flash a series of numbers and letters for a few seconds in front of the class (Examples: EY56Y or 34#$). Ask the students to write them down and describe what they saw. Those students who didn't see or remember the list of random letters or numbers may have visual processing problems. Or may simply not be used to paying attention – or have not found it useful to pay attention.

　　To test auditory perceptions give students a variety of instructions orally and then tell them to carry them out. Example: "when I say go, you will do the following things: stand up sit down put your left hand on your head and your right hand on your desk." Using this, teachers can easily pick out kids who might have learning problems.

2.   **Share goals and expectations**. This has been done in a way that is engaging for most of your students. This is often called a Launch of an activity. Example: A teacher was teaching about missing numbers in patterns. She told the class she had mistakenly washed her pay check in the wash and needed to figure out the missing numbers on the check. She then gave them part of the check and clues for what might be missing. See what engages students. One can also use music or a picture. Make sure cues are meaningful and culturally relevant for the kids you are teaching. Some of them might have never seen checks and only money so you will need a different launch about needing to remember a code on a $20 bill to prove you won the money during a game involving codes that you won with your friends.

3.   **Stimulate prior recall**. To see whether students have already developed some kind of schema in long-term memory as a result of earlier lessons, see if can begin to find a hook on which to attach the concepts in new lessons. Even if students seem to have forgotten everything about your last lesson on desert habitats you are still giving them a context to help learn some new ideas.

4.   **Present in all modalities**. This really works. By pairing a picture or a video or a sound or an action with a new idea there will be more retention in short time memory and more time to keep ideas in short-tem memory when students can interact with them. This is especially helpful for language learning. Wiburg has watched monolingual Spanish speakers who learn words rapidly when given an assignment that connects words to pictures. A sample assignment might be to ask students to develop a presentation on weather using images of types of weather available on the Internet.

5.   **Provide meaningful frameworks**. While, for example, discussing desert animals, provide some frameworks you have used before in learning about animals, which will assist encoding

into an existing schema in the long-term memory. Or even better, provide examples from previous teaching of animals of the desert and ask the students to name them and discuss these animals and then have them construct a meaningful way to classify them.

6.   **Monitor/Adjust Teaching**. Probably the best way to see if students are on board with the lesson so far is to suggest a problem-solving task or project which provides applications for the content and then watch to see who gets it and who doesn't. If they don't seem to be getting it then ask them questions so they can find their way back to the teacher's desired learning goal. Teachers can also have kids help with this by having them ask questions or provide feedback to each other. An elementary school teacher could require kids to ask *three of your peers before me (a strategy introduced by Seymour Papert in his learning work with Logo)* during work time, and only ask the teacher, if three peers didn't have the answer). This is a productive strategy even with graduate students and creates shared responsibility for creating a community of learners.

7.   **Apply.** To see whether students understand a new concept, ask them to apply the idea to some new examples. Teachers will be doing some application in step 6 but those applications should be relatively easy. To see if students have *really* learned something, ask them after they have done simple problems to apply what they have learned to an unfamiliar problem and see what they do.

8.   **Closure**. Just to be sure students understand the lesson for that day, ask them to complete a short task, like writing on a card what they know and using this as an exit card. Or having students tell each other and you what they learned that day. This closure, or debriefing, process really helps with later retrieval of the ideas from long-term memory.

Hopefully this short section on how to work with the brain while teaching will be useful to you.

Why should I learn about brain-based learning?

With our growth in understanding of how our brains work, teachers and designers of lessons and learning environments, have many more strategies to help people learn.

A very simple application is to use powerful pictures, video, sound, and multiple representations of a concept. This strategy will help the learner remember in short-term memory long enough to add new knowledge to long-term memory.

Understanding that when students are fearful a part of their brain is activated that makes it difficult if not impossible to learn, can help teachers and designers to create non-threatening ways to introduce new ideas.

Knowing the long-term memory uses semantics results in presentations and teaching that connects ideas to meaningful images and experiences.

References

Bransford, J., Brown, A. L., Cocking, R. R., & National Research Council (U.S.). (1999). *How people learn: Brain, mind, experience, and school.* Washington, D.C: National Academy Press.

D'Arcangelo, M. (2000). How does the brain develop? A conversation with Steven Petersen. *Educational Leadership, 58*(3), 68-71.

Darling-Hammond, L. & Bransford, J. (2005). *Preparing teachers for a changing world: What teachers should learn and be able to do.* San Francisco, CA: John Wiley & Sons, Inc.

De, G. D. (1975). *Conquest of mind: Phrenology and Victorian social thought.* London: Croom Helm.

Fagan, M. K., Pisoni, D. B., Horn, D. L., & Dillon, C. M. (2007). Neuropsychological correlates of vocabulary, reading, and working memory in deaf children with cochlear implants. *Journal of Deaf Studies and Deaf Education, 12*(4), 461-471.

Heilman, K. M., & Satz, P. (1983). *Neuropsychology of human emotion.* New York: The Guilford Press.

Kenny, A. (1968). *Descartes: A study of his philosophy.* New York: Random House.

Konnikova, M. (2013). The man who couldn't speak—and how he revolutionized psychology. Retrieved from http://blogs.scientificamerican.com/literally-psyched/2013/02/08/the-man-who-couldnt-speakand-how-he-revolutionized-psychology/

Mattison, R. E., Hooper, S. R., & Carlson, G. A. (2006). Neuropsychological characteristics of special education students with serious emotional/behavioral disorders. *Behavioral Disorders*, 176-188.

Thompson, R. F., Berger,T. W., & Berry (1980). An introduction to the anatomy, physiology, and chemistry of the brain. In M. C. Wittrock, *Brain and psychology* (pp. 3-32). New York: Academic Press, Inc.

Vygotsky, L. (1986). *Thought and Language*, trans. A. Kozulin. Cambridge, MA: Harvard University Press.

Chapter 8- Adult Language Learning Theory

Jennifer K. Green

This chapter emphasizes the need for a deviation from K-12 education and the exclusive focus on second language teaching so that all English Language Learners (ELLs) can be successful. English language programs should account for students learning English as a second language but also for those learning English as a third, fourth, or fifth language.

To be critical in teaching means to analyze coursework, to ensure that it highlights issues for isolated communities and dissolves injustice for those groups. TESOL pedagogy needs to transcend primary and secondary education, as more people than ever before have decided to learn English as a new language once they become adults. For this reason, it is important that schooling reduces or even totally eliminates anxiety for learners and programs are adjusted to individual learning styles to honor what students already know and what they need to know.

Sonia Nieto

Sonia Nieto is the Professor Emerita of Language, Literacy, and Culture in the School of Education at the University of Massachusetts, Amherst. Early in her career, Nieto took a job at the first fully bilingual school in the northeastern United States. Her many years teaching students at all grade levels has allowed her to advocate for critical and modern multicultural education. Educators like Nieto have *critical* attitudes to analyze the validity of curricula and ensure that teaching dissolves oppression for marginalized groups. Nieto supports her rationale with the idea that diversity has existed in the United States since its foundation; hence it is practical to think of multicultural education as *basic* education. She reflects, "Multiculturalism is full of conflict, tension, and difference," and certainly it is. These things stitch the world together.

Through her speeches and publications, Nieto coaches future and current educators in their quest for learning techniques that focus on individuality instead of uniformity. This chapter about language learning theory and its application to adult education includes insight from Sonia Nieto's book of 1999, *The Light in Their Eyes: Creating Multicultural Learning Communities*, some of her other publications, and writings from other authors. Nieto takes interest in the education of Latinos, and other culturally and linguistically diverse populations, finding joy in their achievements as equal members of the societies in which they live.

Sonia Nieto's work emphasizes common institutional policies and practices like racism, discrimination, and unbending expectations of students' achievement that create flaws in education systems. Her research promotes teaching as an intellectual and interactive exercise that should be offered to current students to build expertise as critical scholars. She reminds educators that the quality of instruction should not vary based on privilege; in fact, the quality of education should never fluctuate at all. Privileged people identify with a dominant race, social class, and language, and use this power to hold back those with "nonstandard" identities. Nonstandard identities are those that do not follow the ideal behavior and lifestyles of society as a major organization. However, Nieto and her colleague Patty Bode stress that there is a great struggle to create well rounded programs of study within a society and institution with competing messages from academic, political, and popular culture about what is viewed as knowledge and what defines teaching.

Commitment to Language Learning and Understanding Its Purpose

Several dimensions of multicultural education are embedded in language learning processes and theories. Multicultural pedagogy is related to critically redeveloping historical standards, theories, principles, and concepts for language learners of all ages. Like language learning theory, multicultural education affirms issues of identity and differences and confronts issues of power and privilege in society (Nieto & Bode, 2012). Multicultural pedagogy addresses the effect of teacher attitudes and values on student progress. The term *minority* is a label placed on second language learners that sustains a negative undertone and deemphasizes the potential of the group.

In *The Light in Their Eyes: Creating Multicultural Learning Communities*, Sonia Nieto (1999) questions whether teachers can stay committed to overwhelming second language acquisition programs in content areas. Teachers are easily unnerved by the amount of work that goes into designing second language education learning plans. Unfortunately, this means that fewer educators insist on thorough research to better design adult English Language Learner (ELL) programs. Ideally, educators should apply the initial program plans but regularly adjust those programs as they examine cognitive issues through the eyes of the students to fully understand the reasons for high, low, or intermediate English language proficiency (Nieto, 1999). It is important to find out how their native or first language, L1, functions in writing and conversation. It is a good idea to look for words and idioms that vary in tone and have implicit meaning, and to look at common L1 sentence structure. Does the subject come before the verb, or vice versa? Keep in mind that it will be difficult to reshape learned ways of interacting. Nieto (1999) insists that the purpose of research should be to find out how and why a student's native language, culture, deep-rooted attitudes, and childhood education have all influenced motivation and unique learning styles. However, educators sometimes stereotype students when observing them and make inappropriate assumptions. Ethical issues arise in language learning theory, resulting in underdeveloped English language programs, or the belief that no English language acquisition program needs to exist.

Problems With Creating ELL Programs

ELL programs are often created based on the correlations that language education researchers believe to be true (Nieto, 1999). It is important to note that some students are learning English as a second language, while others could be learning it as a third, fourth, or fifth language. It is problematic that many programs focus on the issues that were apparently most important during observational research, and categorize students by their ability and according to what "seems" best for their learning. A program might only minimally meet a student's needs, especially if it is designed for English as a second language when most students are learning it as a tertiary language, for example. Nieto (1999) firmly believes that teachers and tutors truly find out what works best for students as they discover their personalities and backgrounds. She says they can try different teaching approaches to gauge comprehension and promote genuine, organic progress that is not held to institutionalized standards (Nieto, 1999).

Standard curricula do not provide teaching methods that are effective for all learning styles. Policymakers typically turn down proposals for the redesign of English Language Learning to better fit the needs of the students. They claim that "they have already done the research," and pride themselves on the sole completion of an evaluation rather than its successful result. ELL instructor Lizette Román points out that teachers who successfully refine their learning strategies to fit a wide range of learning styles are eager to share improvements with other educators. Unfortunately, these trailblazers are ignored because their techniques do not match the current teaching trend, or might require teachers to complete additional training (Nieto, 1999, p. 83).

The "preview-review" strategy uses the students' first language to develop their English as an additional language (Wright, 2010). The *bilingual* instructor gives a "preview" of what is going to be covered in the source language, teaches the lesson entirely in English, and goes back to the source (native) language at the end to "review" what was taught. Wright (2010) claims that this allows for students to express what they already know about a topic in their first language, making it easier to virtually grasp the same information in English. Students certainly will not understand everything in English, but Wright (2010) points out that they will likely absorb something if the teacher uses the Total Physical Response (TPR) (Asher, 1966). Even so, Wright (2010) disregards the idea that the "preview-review method" is only appropriate if the teacher is bilingual and all students speak the same native language. TPR is a more effective method for speakers of many different native languages who are at multiple stages of language acquisition. Total Physical Response involves matching words with pictures and acting out the meaning of a word so students can easily commit new vocabulary and concepts to memory.

Effective Teaching Methods

Nieto's teaching objectives coincide well with linguist Stephen Krashen's (1982 in Wright, 2010) "natural approach," which categorizes the stages of new language production into four stages: Preproduction, Early Production, Speech Emergence, and Intermediate Fluency. Krashen (1983 in Facella, Rampino, & Shea, 2005) makes an important point that all learners move through these

110

stages in sequential order but may do so at different rates. This idea suggests that a single teaching strategy should be flexible to all the stages of natural acquisition, and in general, multiple strategies should be used to encourage the most progress. Total Physical Response is embedded in the natural approach, as it embraces tactile or hands-on learning and multisensory activities (Facella, Rampino, & Shea, 2005). TPR is utilized more in the Preproduction and Early Production stages, as it stimulates listening and gesture imitation. In the later stages of acquisition, the instructor ideally backs away from role-playing and instead asks students to predict using the questions "how" and "why", while comparing, describing, labeling, listing, graphing, and discussing, and using learned and acquired phrases. The emerging stage prepares students for the Intermediate Fluency stage, which includes writing, critiquing, and analyzing literature and themes to expand discussion and persuade peers to share opinions without much input from the teacher (Facella, Rampino, & Shea, 2005).

Theory of Language Learning

At all levels of the natural approach it is evident that students are required to transcend their current comprehension level by practicing scaffolded simplified English that gradually builds in complexity; Krashen (1982 in Wright, 2010) says that the ability to challenge students while getting them to understand demonstrates the comprehensible input - output process. This means that students can illustrate what the teacher has said (input) and can also produce and effectively communicate their own ideas (output). The natural process of language acquisition happens as a result of the Zone of Proximal Development (ZPD) theory; this concept was originally coined by psychologist Lev Vygotsky (Wright, 2010). The ZPD theory supports the interactive teacher-student relationship that Sonia Nieto recommends as part of critical multicultural education. ZPD highlights the relationship between actual comprehension of problems and concepts on an independent level and potential comprehension with help from the instructor (Wright, 2010). Nieto (1999) advises that teaching methods should be designed around student guidance. The instructor's facilitator role involves smoothing out major misunderstandings for students as they process new information.

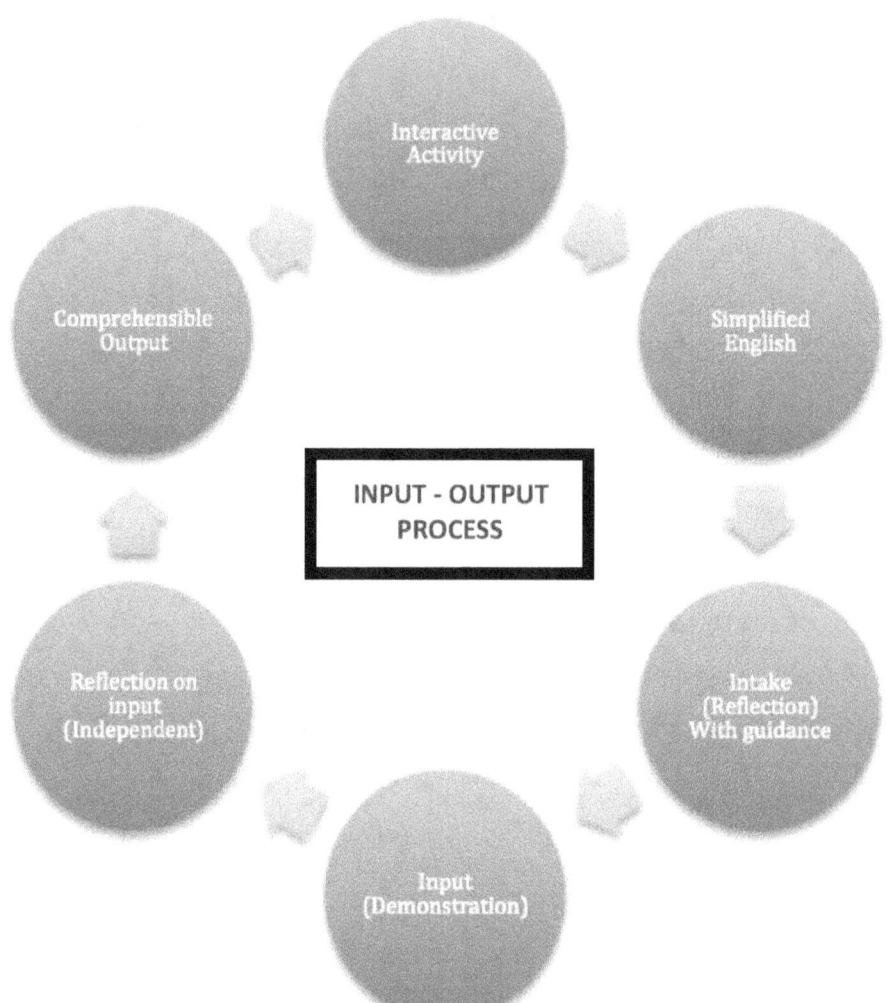

Zoltán Dörnyei, a professor of psycholinguistics at the University of Nottingham in the United Kingdom, supports Nieto's belief that language learning is a social experience that depends on social context. Are students relaxed or anxious in their learning environment? Does the teacher use humor to make presentations fun? Is the teacher bilingual in the source (native) language and in the target (new) language? Is language being learned or acquired? These questions are especially crucial for teaching low- level proficiency adult learners because adults typically absorb a new language more slowly than children. Surprisingly, adults benefit from the same teaching techniques that are used with children (Dörnyei, 2003).

In general, language is *acquired* when it is used subconsciously by watching television, reading books, or talking to native speakers. Language is *learned* when a person tries to understand and master it by carefully examining it in "chunks," without real world context or applications (Freeman & Freeman, 2011). Both adults and children benefit from listening exercises that require repetition of target words in writing and conversation, because speaking, reading, writing, and listening are all interconnected. Speaking and writing are productive processes, while reading and listening are receptive (Peregoy & Boyle, 2013). Low-level proficiency students commonly take more interest in listening than in speaking or writing; they are usually apprehensive to offer their input. To promote their learning, the teacher should guide their conversations so that they talk about their everyday activities. It is helpful to deconstruct "the commute to work," for example; describe the route used to get there, explain how long it takes to get there, and so forth. This technique sparks conversation and reduces anxiety because it requires students to use the amount of language that they know and only introduces them to a few new words at a time.

Stages of Acquisition

Passive Learning (Looking/ Seeing)	Seeing & Hearing	Active Learning (Saying/Doing)

Sonia Nieto and her colleague Patty Bode (2012) note that culturally responsive teachers value students who have been alienated and stereotyped as a result of their status as ELLs. The multicultural perspective is crucial in American society, which is in truth an oligarchy, where an exclusive group of policymakers and politicians enforce the institutionalized "-isms" that infiltrate every aspect of American culture. This type of organization promotes an environment in which any attempt to solve inequality is seen as an attack on deep-rooted cultural values, even though those constructed principles are social and political delusions.

The presence of racism, classism, ableism, and linguicism explains the unease and embarrassment that adult English language learners carry with them every day. The terms *ableism* and *linguicism* might be unfamiliar even for an accomplished scholar. Ableism is discrimination against people with disabilities;

those who do not speak English in the United States are socially impaired and compartmentalized, much like individuals with physical and mental disabilities are ridiculed. Linguicism is discrimination based specifically on language (Adams et al., 2013). Children can be bold and sometimes ignore social cues that they are unwanted in a particular group. Having been more exposed to the social world around them, adults are generally more reluctant to approach social situations in which behavior and language seem unfamiliar to them.

To eliminate these "-isms," it is extremely important to break the cycle of institutional and cultural socialization (Adams et al., 2013). Institutions and dominant cultures bombard their own groups as well as others with messages regarding who should or should not have power in terms of family, health care, criminal justice, policymaking, and education (Adams et al., 2013, p. 46). Without question, the dominant group also decides which languages are acceptable by making a legal distinction between official and unofficial languages. That considered, a student might be afraid to speak English even after hearing classmates speak and being encouraged to practice with them. He or she might not want to make an effort to speak or write for fear of being constantly corrected; ELL students sometimes will express the gnawing feeling that they cannot learn English if it needs fixing all the time (Wright, 2010). This unease stems from the cross-culturally institutionalized idea that teachers are superior to students. This attitude coincides with traditional audiolingual language learning, which centralizes constant error correction and mastery of communication skills through listening (Wright, 2010). This approach, however, damages students' self-confidence.

Communicative learning focuses on *effective* rather than *syntactically correct* communication in the new language (Wright, 2010). If students have the chance to ask questions about the small steps that make up a whole language pattern and can test their dialogue, they also effectively challenge the teacher's knowledge of the language. This reciprocal activity demonstrates that both the teacher and the student play active roles as learners, essentially working off of each other's perspectives. This way, everyone feels less overwhelmed and students largely abandon any doubts they have as they try to apply the in-class conversation models to their everyday interactions.

Application

It makes sense to use technology in the ELL classroom as the current generation of students includes "digital natives" who have grown up with Internet, largely as a form of entertainment. Computer software, applications, and websites enhance listening and conversation with built-in audio and visual aides to advance, reinforce, and assess comprehension. Computer, smartphone, and tablet games might simulate real-life situations that require learners to contemplate the best resolution, or memorize names and characteristics for higher game levels.

Why should I learn about language learning?

Maybe the most important thing to learn about language learning is that language is intertwined with culture and status. Language provides comfort and a feeling of "home."

Good teaching of a language means understanding the native community of the learner. What is this person's first language and what meaning does the home language still have for the learner? Is this person learning more than a second language?

What reasons does the learner have for learning a new language, especially an adult learner?

References

Adams, M., Blumenfeld, W.J., Castañeda, R., Hackman, H.W., Peters, M.L., & Zúñiga, X. (Eds.). (2013). *Readings for diversity and social justice* (3rd ed.). New York, NY: Routledge.

Asher, J. J. (1966). The learning strategy of the total physical response: A review. *The Modern Language Journal, 50*(2), 79-84.

Dörnyei, Z. (2003). Attitudes, orientations, and motivations in language learning: Advances in theory, research, and applications. *Language learning, 53*(S1), 3-32.

Facella, M. A., Rampino, K. M., & Shea, E. K. (2005). Effective teaching strategies for English language learners. *Bilingual Research Journal, 29*(1), 209-221.

Freeman, D. & Freeman, Y. (2011). *Between worlds: Access to second language acquisition* (3rd Ed.). Portsmouth, NH: Heinemann.

Nieto, S. & Bode, P. (2012). *Affirming diversity: The sociopolitical context of multicultural education (6th Ed.).* New York, NY: Longman.

Nieto, S. (1999). *The light in their eyes: Creating multicultural learning communities.* New York, NY: Teachers College Press.

Peregoy, S. F., Boyle, O., & Cadiero-Kaplan, K. (2013). *Reading, writing, and learning in ESL: A resource book for teaching K-12 English learners.* Upper Saddle River, NJ: Pearson Education, Inc.

Wright, W. E. (2010). *Foundations for teaching English language learners: Research, theory, policy & practice.* Philadelphia: Caslon Publishing.

Chapter 9 - The Americans with Disabilities Act and Learning Theory

Gary Bond, J.T. Knight and Brandon McIntire

In 1948, the United Nations promulgated the Universal Declaration of Human Rights, which included a clause that the right to an education is a fundamental (Article 26). In 1954, while the United States Supreme Court fell short of that pronouncement in *Brown v. Board of Education*, 347 U.S. 483 (1954), the court nonetheless found that that *de jure* segregation of school children was "inherently unequal", inequitable, and accordingly unconstitutional. One note to keep in mind that will be discussed in this article on learning for special needs students is that educators have uncovered a common problem: the over-diagnosis and mislabeling of English-as-second-language learners (ELL, *see* Chapter 8) and ethnically non-mainstream students as being learning disabled.

There are at least four interrelated federal statutes relevant to special needs K-12 students in the United States. Whereas Title I of the Elementary and Secondary Education Act of 1965 requires that a certain percentage of families whose children attending a particular school meet minimum threshold poverty levels to qualify for student assistance, the 1975 Individuals with Disabilities Education Act (IDEA), the 1990 Americans with Disabilities Act (ADA), and the 2001 No Child Left Behind Act (NCLB) do not. Each of these legislative frameworks have been amended multiple times.

Taken together, these legal precedents have changed U.S. K-12 and postsecondary education in many ways, from broad changes in instructional design to discrete requirements such as closed-captioning. However, little work has been done on how students with disabilities may be impacted based on a given instructor's learning theory as applied in the classroom, whether face-to-face or online. This chapter's review is limited to viewing entitlement issues through the lens of behavioral, cognitive, and social constructivist learning theories.

Some statutory requirements, such as wheelchair ramps, have no obvious application to learning theories, while others directly relate to a schools' obligation to accommodate students in the least restrictive learning environment possible. A "learning environment" refers to the overall physical and social setting of the classroom, whether at a physical location or online, and decisions about learning environments are predicated on the instructor's chosen learning theories.

Unlike IDEA and SSDI (supplemental security disability income), the ADA does not provide a list of specific disabilities that a person must have in order to qualify for special legal status. Rather, each situation is evaluated on its own merit, including intellectual disabilities, hearing/visual impairments, and traumatic brain injury (TBI)/physiological impairments and dyslexia. *Exceptional Lives: Special Education in Today's Schools* (Turnbull,Turnbull,Wehmeyer,& Shogren, 2013) instructs our understanding of each disability. Individuals with Intellectual Disabilities (ID) each face unique challenges that schools should attempt to diagnose as early as possible in order to maximize intervention tools and techniques that will keep afflicted students from falling to far behind their peers.

Students with intellectual disabilities and traumatic brain injuries

According to Turnbell et al. (2013), individual students with ID may have impairments in short and/or long term memory. They also may exhibit problems generalizing skills they learn in school, and transferring that knowledge to the home setting. In addition to memory and skill transferability, they may also have problems with self-motivation (Turnbell et al., 2013). A given learning environment may either help or hinder students with ID.

Students with dyslexia, for example, are considered to be learning disabled, although their abilities may range widely. Such students have been shown to better understand text printed on a colored (usual pastel) background - the color may depend on the student - as well as text displayed in a specific font (preferably Arial, Comic Sans, Verdana, Tahoma, Century Gothic, or Trebuchet), avoiding ALLCAPS, avoiding underlining or italics, but maintaining specific margins, particular line spacing, and printing on matte paper thick enough so anything on the other side of the page does not show through.

Students with documented traumatic brain injuries (TBI), are often frequently undiagnosed (0.05%) and thus classified as having a TBI, while the estimated prevalence rate is 2.5-4.7% (Schutz, Rivers, McNamara, Schutz, & Lobato, 2010). The presence of TBI may be diagnosed through a simple questionnaire (ibid.). Conversely, diagnosis of an ELL student's learning disability may be quite challenging, as it can entail an evaluation of literacy skills, a verbal assessment of conceptual and vocabulary skills, decoding skills and "phonemic" awareness. As a result, bilingual and minority children may be easily misidentified and placed into special education classes when in fact there is no underlying impairment to warrant that classification.

Behaviorist Theory

Through the lens of a behaviorist theory (see Chapter 2), some ways a teacher can use this approach include positive conditioning (rewarding desired behavior with a treat or a compliment) or negative conditioning (withholding a reward for undesirable behavior). Sometimes behaviorist theory is necessary to stop a behavior that is harmful to a student or others. However after helping the student build new habits other kinds of approaches can be used to help the student become more internally-motivated.

Cognitive Theory

While the feasibility of a cognitive instructional response will be determined by the ability of the student, there are instructional strategies that can inform teachers on how to assist students with special needs to utilize their short-term and long-term cognitive strategies. For example having a student create a project using preferred modalities like building objects or connecting ideas to music can help with longer learning retention. Teachers should be assisted to use these strategies in order to attempt an inclusive learning process. The teacher will have to choose among appropriate assistive tools.

Social Constructivist Theory

With a social constructivist approach, teachers still must determine the strengths and weaknesses of any given student, and then attempt to construct a group learning environment perhaps focusing on the strengths of students with special needs. Sometimes students with special needs are especially patient and helpful in assisting younger students to learn basic skills like learning to read. As mentioned, a teacher must be fully aware of any means that are available in order to adapt, improvise, and construct a least restrictive environment, yet provide guided support. This will be a continuous and ongoing process.

The applied behaviorist, cognitive and social constructivist approaches provided above are applicable to all students with special needs under the ADA, as adapted to each student as circumstances warrant.

Hearing Loss

Students with hearing loss impairment may have loss of spoken language (Turnbell et al., 2013). Sometimes teachers confuse what they perceive as a loss as related to the students intelligence or thinking, *Oh he can't hear so he can't do this complex project*. However, the IQ range of students with hearing loss is pretty much the same as the general population of students. Because of this, students with hearing loss would only require minor assistance within their limitations, in order to fully incorporate them into a regular learning environment. Generally, positive reinforcement provides extra encouragement that a person with hearing loss can benefit from. It would also be helpful to understand the student's written and spoken language losses as a result of hearing loss and help remediate any loses found by building new skills with the student.

Visual Impairments (VI)

A large portion of traditional teaching relies on visual cues, and without them, students with Visual Impairments (VI) have difficulty learning (Turnbell et al., 2013). Students with VI may require extra opportunities to explore, comprehend, and understand; they may also have difficulty fully sharing common experiences. Individuals with VI also have an increased problem with mobility, since their loss of sight precludes them from traveling (ibid.).

Positive reinforcement provides a good approach when working within a behaviorist approach. The teacher should provide as much specific feedback as possible to the visually-impaired students and praise him or her for their compensating strategies. Phrases such as "I noticed you are writing down a list of things to do in this assignment" can be excellent approaches for encourage a student with a VI.

Physical Disabilities (PD)

According to Turnbell et al. (2013) and IDEA, students with Physical Disabilities (PD) have an "orthopedic impairment," and may exhibit difficulties with their educational processes. Some examples of students with PD are cerebral palsy and spina bifida. **Several diagnostic tools are available for each of the aforementioned impairments**

So far, this book has addressed various strategies for educating students, some of whom may be learning-impaired for one reason or another. The age of the student should also be considered since adult brain activities may be quite different from the brain activities of developing students. An understanding of developmental learning theory is also necessary for educators interested in designing optimal learning environments for learning disabled students.

Why should I learn about learning disabilities?

Probably the most important thing to understand about any kind of physical of intellectual disability is that they do not have to be a serious barrier to learning. Teachers and educational leaders can use what we know about learning theory and the nature of disabilities to design effective strategies so these students can reach as much of their potential as possible.

There are many useful ways to compensate for any disability and to support each person in their desired to learn.

References

Schutz, L. E., Rivers, K. O., McNamara, E., Schutz, J. A., &
     Lobato, E. J. (2010). Traumatic Brain Injury in K-12
     Students: Where Have All the Children
     Gone?. *International Journal of Special Education*,*25*(2),
     55-71.

Turnbull, A., Turnbull, H., Wehmeyer, M., & Shogren, K. (2013).

     Exceptional lives: Special education in today's schools

     (7th ed.). Upper Saddle River, NJ: Merrill.

Chapter 10 - Organizational Learning

Gary Bond & Laura Carrillo

Over centuries, learning theory has focused on pedagogy, which is commonly defined as the art and science of teaching children. Knowles explains that shortly after World War I some learning theorists began to argue for differentiation between adult and child learning. Malcolm Knowles highlights how many ancient cultures were also concerned with the outcomes of adult education, yet very little work had been done on the process of adult learning (Knowles, 1984). With this established, Knowles begins a review of background work on which his book, *The Adult Learner: A Neglected species*, is based.

Malcolm Knowles

Dr. Malcolm Knowles (1913-1997) claims there are two streams of learning research, one based on rigorous and traditional (positivistic) scientific methods, based primarily on the work of Edward L. Thorndike. The other is "the artistic stream, which seeks to discover new knowledge through intuition and the analysis of experience", Knowles argues that "this second stream is especially relevant to "*how* adults learn" (1984, p. 28). Knowles' argument begins with the work of Eduard C. Linderman's *The Meaning of Adult Education,* published in 1926. Knowles extensively cites Linderman, highlighting the importance of linking learning and doing, and suggesting that "experience is the adult learner's living textbook", and that teachers of adults should "also be searchers after wisdom and not oracles" (1984, p. 29). Knowles consolidates Linderman's work into six key assumptions (noted below), and further explores other advocates of adult learning theory. There are two statements that stand out as adding clarity to Knowles' theory. The first is from Robert D. Leigh, whom he cites for the proposition that "[t]here is gradually emerging, therefore, a conception of education as a lifelong process beginning at birth and ending only with death" (1984, p. 33). The second is Wendell Thomas, who said, "adult education is as different from ordinary schooling as adult life ... is different from the protected life of the child" (Knowles, 1984, p. 36).

Another group of researchers that have added substantially to Knowles work are those working in Adult Education, especially Cyril O. Houle and Allen Tough. Houle's research found that adult's choose to engage in learning activities based on being either *goal-oriented*, such as working toward a degree, *activity-oriented*, who use learning to engage in social activities, and *learning-oriented*, which are those who engage in learning for the growth the activity offers . Tough's work was focused on determining not only "what and why adults learn, but how they learn and what help they obtain for learning" (Knowles, 1984, p. 45). He found that adults generally organize their learning based on projects and that adults can spend as much as 700 hours a year on learning activities.

While Knowles has sometimes been credited with coining the term "andragogy", Knowles himself gave credit to Alexander Kapp in 1833, a German grammar school teacher (Knowles, 1984, p. 49). Knowles contrasts andragogy from "the pedagogical model [which] assigns to the teacher full responsibility for making all decisions about what will be learned, how it will be learned, when it will be learned, and if it has been learned" (Knowles,1984, p. 52).

Knowles believes these principles are counter to the developing self-identity being developed as a child matures through adolescence and into adulthood, creating a "gap between the need and the ability to be self-directing, and this produces tension, resistance, resentment and often rebellion in the individual" (ibid.). In an attempt to help resolve this conflict, Knowles created the andragogical model.

The Andragogical Model

The andragogical model of learning theory is comprised of six assumptions about the qualities of an adult learner. An understanding of each can lead to creating an environment in which adult learner can thrive. These six assumptions are focused on the same concepts as the pedagogical definition; however, they explain how an adult learner is not the same as a young student.

1. **The need to know**. Adults need to know why they need to learn something before undertaking to learn it. Consequently, one of the new aphorisms in adult education is that the first task of the facilitator of learning is to help the learner become aware of "the need to know." Some of the better tools for raising the level of awareness of the need to know are real or simulated experiences in which the learners discover for themselves the gaps between where they are now and where they want to be. Experiences can help adult learners decide what they need to know.

2. **The learners' self-concept**. Adults have a self-concept of being responsible for their own decisions, for their own lives. They resent and resist situations in which they feel others are imposing their wills on them. This presents a serious challenge to educators of adults: the minute they walk into an act labeled as "education" or "training", they may retreat back into a student mode as conditioned by prior school experience, and expect to be passively lectured to.

3. **The role of learners' experience**. Adults come into an educational activity with both a greater volume and a different quality of experience than the teacher. This difference in quality and quantity of experience has several consequences for adult education. Not only does it assure that in any group of adults there will be a wider range of individual differences than is the case with K-12 students, but it also means that for many kinds of learning the richest source of learning resides in the adult learners themselves. Hence, the greater emphasis in adult education is on experiential techniques-such as group discussion, simulation exercises, problem-solving activities, case method, and laboratory methods.

4. **Readiness to learn**. Adults become ready to learn those things they need to

know and be able to do in order to cope effectively with real-life situations. It is not necessary to sit by passively and wait for readiness to develop naturally, however. There are ways to induce readiness through exposure to models of superior performance, career counseling, simulation exercises, and other techniques.

5. **Orientation to learning**. In contrast to children and youth, adults are life-centered in their orientation to learning. Adults are motivated to devote energy to learning something to the extent that they perceive that it will help them perform tasks or deal with problems they confront in their life situations. Furthermore, new knowledge, understandings, skills, values, and attitudes are most effectively learned when they are presented in the context of application to real-life situations.

6. **Motivation**. While adults are responsive to some external motivators (better jobs, promotions, higher salaries, and the like), the most potent motivators are internal pressures (the desire for increased job satisfaction, self-esteem, quality of life, and the like) (Knowles, 1984).

Future and application of andragogy

It should be noted that Knowles did not address cognitive and social constructivist learning theories, perhaps anticipating future developments in educational theory. Knowles (1984) states

> *the andragogical model, as I see it, is not an ideology; it is a system of alternative sets of assumptions. And this leads us to the critical difference between the two models. The andragogical model is a system of assumptions which includes the pedagogical assumptions. (p. 62).*

While the pedagogical model Knowles identifies is still in use, many of its assumptions have been modified and are now closer to the andragogical assumptions Knowles endorsed. Problem-centered learning, contextualization of material, teacher as facilitator, and the appreciation of experience brought to the classroom, whether through cultural or experiential learning, are now common topics of discussion in the pedagogical arena.

Many examples of how Knowles' assumptions are implemented can be found in the current age. Look no further than the myriad of websites that allow the independent learner to self-select and guide their own learning. For example, when a tool of modern life – such as a washing machine - is having problems, one can use the Internet to readily identify and diagnose the problem, order the appropriate parts, and find videos explaining the repair process. In this example, the individual recalls any previous experience, is able to understand the need to learn, is self-directed in learning, and thus motivated by his or her internal drive to overcome the problem and gain self-satisfaction.

The value of this theory is evident in how (it could be argued under the guise of new pedagogy) the assumptions have been integrated into current discussions about learning theory. Knowles was correct in his statement that all learners could benefit from the type of learning he advocates.

Adult learning is an integral part of facilitating learning in any organization however is not sufficient for addressing the challenges in organizations. What is needed is a systems approach that looks at the entire organization and its parts and can work towards facilitating organizational learning.

Like Knowles, Peter Senge contributed to organizational learning, but by placing collective human values, rather than just self-interest, at the cornerstone of the workplace (Senge, 2006).

Peter Senge

Dr. Peter Senge has been credited with pioneering the concept of systems thinking in business (Fodness., D., 2005). He holds a B.S. in engineering from Stanford University, and an S.M. in social systems modeling as well as a PhD in management from MIT. Dr. Senge is currently a lecturer in the department of Leadership and Sustainability at the MIT Sloan School of Management (Senge, 2015). His emphasis is on the decentralization and distribution of the leadership role in businesses and organizations to empower employees in an effort to improve employee's capabilities in order to work toward a common goal.

Peter Senge is broadly known for his book T*he Fifth Discipline, The Art and*

131

Practice of the Learning Organization. This book became a 7 volume series in which he attributes the creation of "organizations that learn" to the integration of the 5 "learning disciplines" (Senge, 2006). In addition, Senge is the founding chair of SoL, the Society for Organizational Learning, an institution which is dedicated to the advancement of people and the organizations of which they are a part.

Senge made the concept of a 'learning organization" popular in his first edition of *The Fifth Discipline* book, however, it was Chris Argyris, who first used the term "learning organization". Argyris, known as "The Father of Organizational Learning", had more than 3 decades of experience in the field before his death in 2013. Argyris, in his book, *Integrating the Individual and the Organization*, examines institutions in an effort to analyze what elements hinder success and which factors enable it. Senge, clearly an innovator in his time, has built upon the foundation that Argyris set down. The disciplines of personal mastery and a shared vision help persons and groups of individuals envision a goal and set the course to reach those goals. The two disciplines that follow focus on individual and collective reflection in an effort to reach a desired objective. The final discipline deals with systematic change and the intricacies of the effects of singular actions and its far-reaching effects on an organization (Senge, 2015).

Senge's Learning Theory

Human values in the workplace are the foundation expressed in Senge's work. His design promotes the idea that organizations can realize their potential through a shared vision, purpose, reflection, and the use of systems thinking (Senge, 2015). He stresses the importance of an all-inclusive methodology to business and organizational approaches (Fodness, 2005).

The five disciplines that are required to create organizational learning are listed below.

Table 3: The Five Disciplines

Discipline	Description
Personal Mastery	The development of your own personal vision. The alignment of what you most desire with a true evaluation of your current reality. This creates an accessible gap between the need to achieve and the achievable.
Shared Vision	This discipline creates a common purpose for those in the organization or school. With a collective purpose, the individuals involved foster a sense of commitment and are guided by common goals and strategies to achieve these objectives. This shared vision must come from all of the stakeholders in an organization.
Mental Models	This discipline focuses on reflection and cognizance of one's own attitudes and the attitudes of others. This can help create a clearer perspective of reality.
Team Learning	Dialogue is key for this group activity. This discipline, through the exchange of ideas helps individuals utilize their skills to accomplish one unifying goal.
Systems Thinking	This discipline deals with the interdependency within an organization and helps people better understand the magnitude and effect of their individual actions on the entire system.

Senge notes that fundamentally, the root cause of problems in an organization is caused by the relationships and mental models used in that organization (Senge, Cambron-McCabe, Lucas, Smith, & Dutton, 2012). The five disciplines of organizational learning are meant to cultivate leadership as well and cooperation and to enhance awareness of the frames of mind that direct behavior and mold organizational structure (Senge et al, 2012).

The Five Disciplines

The first two disciplines set the course by aligning the goals of the individual with the goals of the organization. Personal mastery examines the needs of the individual and connects personal desire to an attainable organizational goal. Shared vision necessitates focusing on a common objective, wherein people have a common goal and develop a sense of commitment. For an organization to expect to thrive, the individuals must commit to a shared vision (Senge et al, 2012).

The next two disciplines encourage reflective thinking for the individual and the group. Understanding Mental models focuses on reflection about your own attitudes and the attitudes of those around you, while team learning encourages you to share those observations with other members in an effort to transform their thinking and attain common goals for both the good of the individual and the organization.

The final of the five disciplines is systems thinking. Systems thinking has the power to create the most productive change in an organization. In order to do so, people must begin to recognize the interdependency of the parts of an institution, thereby giving all of the stakeholders insight into how their own individual actions affect the entire system. Research on systems thinking demonstrates that even small changes, when properly focused, can cause great and lasting change (Senge, 1990). Senge asks readers to look to themselves as contributors to the problem and as part of the potential solution. He asks the individual to reflect on the ways their own actions are influencing and playing a roll in the organizational problems (Senge, 2015).

Senge describes 4 steps in identifying and beginning to solve the root cause of an issue. The first step is identifying a specific event, such as a low graduation rate. People react to each of these instances as if they were separate and react to treat the problem as an isolated event instead of looking at all of the factors or events that could be related. The next step is to graph the events that may be related to this issue and assess the patterns that may be emerging. Events like getting a new principal and a jump in enrollment may seem unrelated, however, patterns will begin to appear. It is rare to find a pattern that has not come up previously. Next, the elements that contribute to these changes in behavior patterns are analyzed, including how seemingly unrelated factors interrelate. In order to be able to make systematic change, it is crucial to be able to understand the current organization and its practices. However, the step, mental models, can be seen as the most important element to systematic change since these structures and their practices are shaped by the values, attitudes and deeply held principles of those in them (Senge, 2015).

The five disciplines are the staple of Senge's book, *Schools That Learn, a Fifth Discipline Resource, A Fifth Discipline Fieldbook For Educators, Parents, and Everyone Who Cares About Education* along with his other six books in the "The Fifth Discipline" series. Senge's main philosophical premise is based on the thought that organizations are a product of their member's thoughts and interactions (Senge et al, 2012). The strengths and weaknesses of an organization in Senge's theory rely on one main factor: the individuals within it. Senge is cited in many academic works about organizational learning theory and systems learning and is a leader in his field, however, there are those who disagree with some of his contentions.

Some argue that cultivating an individual's need to align with the vision of the institution is exploitive. For example, Esterby-Smith and his colleagues contend that such alignment and modification of individual behavior toward the vision of the management necessarily leads to a regulation of the members of the organization (Easterby-Smith, Araujo, & Burgoyne, 1999). This arrangement is mutually beneficial for the reason that it helps individuals guide their own personal goals and take pride in the changes they contribute to in their institutions.

But individuals can also be resistant to and indeed thwart change. However, if learning is driven by vision, and that vision can in-fact be tapped into, there are no limits to the progress that both an individual and an organization can make, for in the vision, lies the most crucial aspect to success (Senge et al, 2012).

Application

As an illustrative hypothetical, let us say that a high school principal conducts a meeting every Monday, Wednesday and Friday during 4th period to discuss student projects and assessments (both formative and summative), receive professional development, and to disseminate important information to each department. Another individual, the department head, introduces the principal, who then states *with the changing graduation requirements we have the opportunity to build a dream. No longer do we need to adhere to the same cookie-cutter plan for every student. With our new plan, students are able to meet the requirements for certain prerequisite courses, then, in their junior and senior years, students can choose what they are interested in, while completing their high school requirements. Imagine being able to teach, what you are most passionate about, to be able to teach to students who chose your class because they too are passionate and interested in learning what you want to teach.*

Teachers begin chatting amongst themselves, exchanging a few ideas as a few faces light up as they ponder the possibilities. One teacher expresses "I have always loved agriculture. I took many courses in my undergrad coursework. I would love to be able to teach Biotech. We can start a garden and even a salad bar. . ." she trails off as she considers the possibilities and begins to envision her students engaged in projects that better the community.

The principal responds, "that's what I'm talking about! And it's not only in science, but also in all the core classes. If you can put the work in, we can help provide support for you. Together we can build this school into the type of school that every student wants to be a part of. Now, what about other among you? What are you interested in pursuing?"

This short scenario provides a good opportunity to discuss why we care so much about learning and its implications for constituents beyond teachers and administrators.

Why should I learn about organizational learning?

So often in education well-meaning folks are advocating what they think are the best ways to educate students. However they often pull and plan in opposite directions, so that educational change turns into a tug-of-war and nothing is accomplished.

If members of a group can agree to pull together in one direction, a great deal more can be accomplished. The key is understanding how systems work and learn and then implementing change in the systems you care about in ways that align with each other.

References

Knowles, M. (1984). *The adult learner: A neglected species (3rd ed.).* Houston, TX: Gulf Publishing.

Argyris, C. (1964). *Integrating the individual and the organization.* New York: Wiley.

Easterby-Smith, M., Araujo, L., & Burgoyne, J. (1999). *Organizational learning and the learning organization: Developments in theory and practice.* London: Sage Publications.

Fodness, D. (2005). Rethinking strategic marketing: achieving breakthrough results. *Journal of Business Strategy, 26*(3), 20-34.

Senge, P. M. (1990). *The fifth discipline: The art and practice of the learning organization.* New York: Doubleday/Currency.

Senge, P. M. (2006). *The fifth discipline: The art and practice of the learning organization.* New York: Doubleday/Currency.

Senge, P. M., Cambron-McCabe, N., Lucas, T., Smith, B., & Dutton, J. (2012). *Schools that learn (updated and revised): A fifth discipline fieldbook for educators, parents, and everyone who cares about education.* Crown Business.

Senge, P., (2015) Bibliography of Peter Senge, Senior Lecturer, Leadership and Sustainability. Retrieved from http://mitsloan.mit.edu/faculty/

Chapter 11- Why is it Important for People to Learn about Learning?
Whole Class Reflections

Learning how to learn is a metacognitive ability that as far as we know, is unique to human beings. Its importance has been recognized since ancient times and for a number of reasons.

One reason why it is important to understand learning theory is to be able to reach as many students as possible by tailoring instruction to particular learners using learning strategies such as using different modalities, or building multiple synapse-connecting pathways to best foster retention and interdisciplinary application. While learning is a reciprocal and lifelong process, well-prepared students ideally are able to move toward becoming independent learners.

Another related reason is that education can be - and in Western countries, is - the bedrock foundation of democracy as reflected by the individualism embraced by John Dewey. However, as Dewey warned, education can also be 'misused' and become the founding principles of a dictatorship, oligarchy, theocracy or anarchy. Examples of such dysfunctional systems can be seen in novels such as *Fahrenheit 451*, *Animal Farm*, and the *Fountainhead*, and such films as 2001: *A Space Odyssey*, *A Clockwork Orange*, and *Ex Machina*.

Democratic ideals may be further advanced when politicians, policy makers, and stakeholders such as parents and students know something about how and why learning works, and which methods work best and under what environmental conditions. The careful reader should take note that this book endorses experiential learning styles, self- and group-based assessments over simply lecturing, assigning homework and then testing students for content knowledge. We waste precious educational resources in test preparation that could otherwise be used to facilitate environmental learning and use cognitive diagnostic tools to alert teachers when and where early intervention is appropriate. Policy makers will benefit by gaining a theoretical perspective that focuses more on student learning rather than teacher testing. Questioning the underlying theoretical framework that may or may not comprise educational institutions require a strong foundation based out of educational research and proven theory.

The future of education, one which is increasingly driven by a focus on technology, has already arrived. Technological platforms, such as phones and tablets, can make education available to everyone. But we still need to prepare students for how to use them and how to assess their potential critically.

Our hope is that this book will contribute to these discussions by making multiple educational theories accessible to, and interesting for, the average reader.

This book was written by the students in EDLT and EDUC 607, a merged class on learning, research, and technology in the Department of Curriculum & Instruction at New Mexico State University. The doctoral students will save any monies earned by this book in a fund to support future publications and presentations. If you would like to comment on any parts of this book, please send your comments to Dr. Karin Wiburg at kwiburg@nmsu.edu, or to

Jennifer Green at jkgreen@nmsu.edu .

ABOUT THE EDITORS

Karin Wiburg, Ed.D. is a distinguished professor of Learning Design and Technology in the Department of Curriculum and Instruction in the College of Education at New Mexico State University. She has been at NMSU for 23 years and served as the Associate Dean for Research for nine of those years. She has written several books and many articles and is often invited to present on learning and technology. She was the professor for this class.

Julia Lynn Parra, EdD, is an Assistant Professor at New Mexico State University. She codesigned and teaches for NMSU's Online Teaching and Learning Graduate Certificate Program and is the coordinator for the Learning Design & Technology programs. Her research interests include the interactions between learning design, technology, innovation, and culturally relevant teaching and learning. She has published and presented on professional development in online teaching and learning for teachers in K12 education, the creation of a course design model for cloud-based student collaboration, digital explorations along the borderlands, technology-based projects for empowering marginalized populations, and innovative models and strategies for designing learning environments such as the use of HyFlex and conducting the first MOOC at NMSU. Prior to receiving her Ed.D. in Learning Technologies from Pepperdine University, she was a middle school teacher with Las Cruces Public Schools. Her email is juparra@nmsu.edu

Gaspard Mucundanyi is a Ph.D student in Curriculum and Instruction with a specialization in educational learning technologies at NMSU. He holds a Master of Science in Engineering and a Bachelor's degree in Information Technology. He taught computer science courses at different universities in Rwanda for seven years and worked as officer in charge of multimedia contents in the National Curriculum Development Centre, Rwanda, for four years. His research interests focus on online learning and teaching, social network , instructional design, and *gamification*. His email is mucundanyi@gmail.com.

Jennifer Green recently completed her TESOL Masters degree candidate and works teaching English to international students at New Mexico State University. Her research primarily aims to uncover action methods for dissolving linguistic discrimination, challenging unequal social stratification based on language, and empowering adults who are working toward new language acquisition in regions throughout the world including Spain and the United States. She a B.A. in Spanish from Eastern Connecticut State University as well as a masters in TESOL from New Mexico State University. Her email is jkgreen@nmsu.edu.

Nathaniel Shaver is a Sport Psychology and Curriculum & Instruction Ph.D. student at New Mexico State University. Nate specializes in the development and application of teaching models that emphasize skill acquisition and replication. With a passion for athletic performance, specifically baseball, Nate utilizes his knowledge to promote an effective learning environment through coaching. He also holds a M.S. degree in Biology and a B.S. with an emphasis in Wildlife Management & Spanish.

ABOUT THE CONTRIBUTERS

Gary Bond is an Instructional Coordinator and New Mexico State University Alamogordo where he works with faculty to design online courses and is the Quality Matters™ Coordinator. He is a doctoral student in Curriculum & Instruction where he is focusing his work on Accessibility in online courses.

Wanda Bulger-Tamez is the director of the Mathematically-Connected Communities program and is a co-director of the STEM Research and Partnerships group at NMSU. She is a doctoral student studying mathematics education and bilingual education . She has worked for over 20 years at NMSU.

Pamela Duncan is currently a pursing a Ph.D. in Education at New Mexico State University – Las Cruces. Her focus is on Learning Technologies in the Curriculum and Instruction department. She is interested in the integration of technology within math curricula. Pamela wants to find more effective ways of teaching mathematics that increase content retention, especially at the middle school and high school level. She has earned a B.A. in Elementary Education from Arizona State University and a M.A. in Mathematics Education from Western Governors University.

Laura Carrillo is a school administrator of Irvine High School in El Paso Independent and is interested in facilitating project-based learning in her school. As assistant principal she also facilitates the community of learning work at her school. She is a doctoral student in Curriculum and Instruction.

Cynthia Gomez is an educator of 19 years within public education. She has 10 years experience as an administrator and 8 years as an elementary teacher and has recently been hired at New Mexico State University as the Senior Project Manager for an NSF-funded project called Math Snacks (math games and inquiry for math learning). She earned her Bachelor's degree in Elementary Education with a minor in English, a Masters of Arts degree in Educational Management and Development, and a graduate minor in ESL. She is currently gaining a PHD in the area of Educational Distance Learning and Technology with a minor in Educational Leadership and Development.

Brandon McIntire is a graduate assistant in the department of Special Education. He is a doctoral student in Special Education, where he is focusing his studies on inclusionary perspectives of students with disabilities.

Mehmet Özer studied systems of Turkish Language in Turkey for four years and obtained a masters degree on teaching Turkish language. He worked five years as a teacher in Turkey and two years in Texas public schools. Currently he is working on his PhD. studies on curriculum and instruction at New Mexico State University